TOM LAWTON'S

WALKING AROUND

THE PEAK DISTRICT

TOM LAWTON'S
WALKING AROUND
THE PEAK
DISTRICT

A 10-stage, long-distance
walking route through the
White and Dark Peaks

Photographs by the author
Maps and diagrams by
William Rouse

WARD LOCK

DEDICATION

This book is dedicated to the carefree youngsters of today who delight in walking through our National Parks and who will grow up to become the formidable future guardians of this most precious outdoor heritage.

OUTDOOR WRITERS' GUILD – GUIDE-LINES

The long-distance walking route described in this book complies with the guide-lines for writers of path guides issued by The Outdoor Writers' Guild.

Based upon the Ordnance Survey mapping with the permission of the Controller of Her Majesty's Stationery Office © Crown copyright.

A WARD LOCK BOOK

First published in the UK 1995
by Ward Lock, Wellington House, 125 Strand
LONDON WC2R 0BB

A Cassell Imprint

Copyright © Tom Lawton and William Rouse 1995

Distributed in the United States
by Sterling Publishing Co., Inc.
387 Park Avenue South, New York, NY 10016-8810

Distributed in Australia
by Capricorn Link (Australia) Pty Ltd
2/13 Carrington Road, Castle Hill NSW 2154

A British Library Cataloguing-in-Publication Data block for this book may be obtained from the British Library

ISBN 0 7063 7247 6
Typeset by Litho Link Ltd, Welshpool, Powys, Wales
Printed & bound in Slovenia by Printing House DELO-Tiskarna
by arrangement with Korotan Ljubljana

Previous page: *Above Mill Dale*

CONTENTS

PREFACE

The passion and love of my youth for walking in the Peaks was re-kindled during researches for my walking guide, *Exploring the Peak District*. In the variety of its landscape the region is unique amongst upland areas of this country: wild, acid moorlands, peat bogs, isolated tors and endless gritstone edges surround and merge with gentler limestone slopes covered with lush grass. These pastures are intermittently ripped apart by deep gorges displaying rock forms of every shape and size. Small, merry streams drain vast catchment landscapes and finally deposit their contents into the more placid rivers below, flowing between tree-fringed banks in wide valleys or in narrow dales. Where else could you find such a perfect countryside?

The varied and pleasing topography of the Peak District National Park could have been sculptured especially for long-distance walking and therefore a guide-book to this region was the obvious follow-up to my first long-distance route described in *Walking the Lakeland Round*. The interest in such routes has grown tremendously in recent years, and high amongst the reasons for this is that completely new areas of countryside can be explored on each successive day. During the intervening evenings there is the pleasure of talking through the day's experiences with walking companions and planning new delights and challenges for the morrow. This is the perfect relaxing end to each day's physical exertions.

Like the Lakeland Round, the long-distance walk around the Peak is a challenging one of 10 stages. Each stage may be completed by a choice of alternative ways that range from routes providing suitable goals for the very strongest and fittest hill walkers, to variants ideally suited to the more modest capabilities of the rest of us. From the alternatives suggested for each stage, the walking party will be able to select an overall route that will almost certainly be unique but that will hold to the original concept and remain within an accepted time-frame for trekking round the Dark and White Peaks, using the same overnight stopping locations.

Whatever series of options you decide to string together in completing this walk, I wish you well with your individual exploration. Enjoy your adventure to the full and have a safe and immensely enjoyable journey.

T.L.

AUTHOR'S ACKNOWLEDGEMENTS

It gives me pleasure to record my gratitude to the many kind people who have contributed to this book. They have given generously of both their precious leisure time and expertise to make this latest walking guide possible. To all those concerned, please accept my warm appreciation and sincere thanks for your efforts and for the agreeable way you did this.

My special thanks are due to several friends and walking companions of long standing who accompanied me on various stages of the walk. In particular Bob Carter, with his immense knowledge of the Peak District, was a tower of strength and a wise counsellor. I found an agreeable new companion in Mike Horrox, who shared some of the walking stages with me. Bill Rouse made his usual immaculate contribution to the design and production of the innovative computer diagrams, whilst Bob Carter and Eddie Fidler meticulously checked my draft manuscript and verified the proof stages of the book. Ian Morris continued to keep my computer systems running and upgraded with state-of-the-art technology.

May I also express my appreciation to the knowledgeable Rangers of the Peak National Park for checking through the text of the 10 walking stages and for their guidance and constructive advice.

This was arranged through Roland Smith, Head of Information Services, and I am also indebted to Roly for additional contributions, including information on addresses and transport services.

I talked to many fellow walking enthusiasts and these agreeable exchanges of views and experiences between people who share a common bond stimulated my endeavours and gave further purpose and direction to my efforts. Their comments and helpful suggestions are much appreciated. On these travels I came into contact with more than the usual number of youngsters, who proved a delight to talk to. This is acknowledged further in my dedication.

Finally, I express my thanks and gratitude to my wife, Bridget, and also to my two daughters, Katrina and Helen, who continued to accept competition for my time and attention during the compilation of this book and who always provided the most agreeable support for my efforts and on occasions even pampered to my demands.

CONCEPT OF THE ROUTE AND USING THE BOOK

Walks in the Peak District, as in most other upland areas of the United Kingdom, are usually completed within a day. These routes are circuitous: the walkers return to their starting location. When suitable transport is available, they have more freedom to choose linear routes and might finish a hike many kilometres away from their starting point, having trekked over continually varying terrain for the entire walk.

The concept of adding together individual linear walks of convenient daily length to form attractive and demanding long-distance walking routes has grown in popularity in recent years, particularly since the opening of the Pennine Way. Walkers are increasingly attracted to these long-distance ways and obtain immense pleasure and satisfaction in completing them within target time-frames. However, the problem remains that starting and ending points are many kilometres apart and that the possibilities for commencing extended linear walks from convenient intermediate points are strictly limited.

Walking the Lakeland Round is my guide to a long-distance route in the Lakeland Fells which overcame these constraints in that it was devised as a long-distance *circular* walk, of 10 separate stages, which could be started at any point along the way – usually from a designated overnight stopping place. From the chosen starting point the Round could be walked either way, clockwise or anti-clockwise. The Lakeland Round has since become a popular long-distance walk, attracting many determined walkers from all age groups.

Following the success of the Lakeland Round, the second long-distance route in this series is a similar walk around the Peak District. It incorporates the many innovative features included in *Walking the Lakeland Round*, suitably adapted to the different terrain of the Peak. It also includes suggestions and positive feedback based on the experiences of walkers who have undertaken the Lakeland Round and want more of the same.

ARRANGEMENT

This challenging long-distance route consists of several very flexible alternative ways so that walkers of most age groups and of varying fitness levels and abilities can really enjoy trekking over the acid moorlands and gritstone edges of the Dark Peak and across the meadowlands and the spectacular limestone dales and gorges of the White Peak. They can select a circuit that best suits individual needs from the alternatives described for each of the 10 separate stages of the walk. For most walkers the ideal route might be one that is demanding for them but at the same time is well within their physical and mental capabilities; other walkers will have different priorities, and these will be reflected in the combination of alternatives that each walker selects. Groups with mixed abilities may split up to follow their own route variants during the day, then meet up again in the evening.

Approaching Higger Tor

THE COMPLETE ROUTE

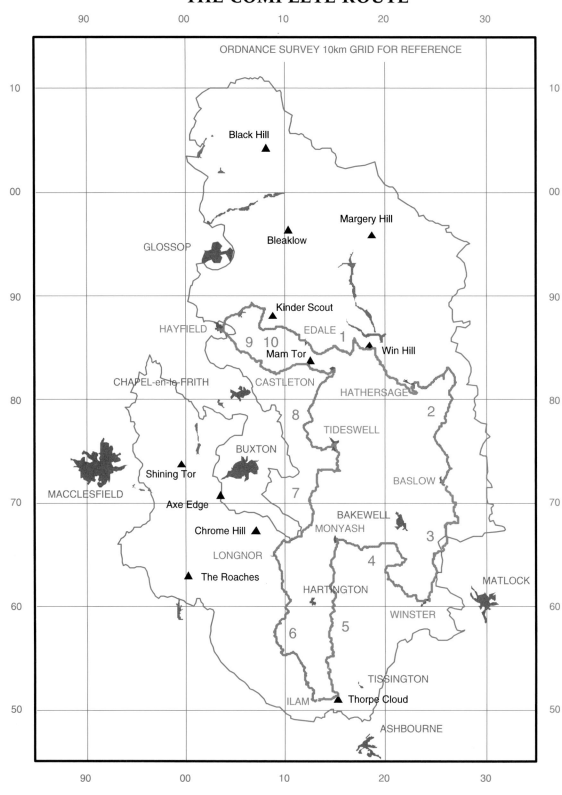

ORDNANCE SURVEY 10km GRID FOR REFERENCE

Black Hill ▲

Margery Hill ▲

Bleaklow ▲

GLOSSOP

Kinder Scout ▲

HAYFIELD   EDALE   1

9   10

Mam Tor ▲   Win Hill ▲

CHAPEL-en-le-FRITH   CASTLETON

HATHERSAGE

8   2

TIDESWELL

BUXTON

Shining Tor ▲   BASLOW

MACCLESFIELD   Axe Edge ▲   7

BAKEWELL   3

Chrome Hill ▲   MONYASH

LONGNOR   4

MATLOCK

The Roaches ▲   HARTINGTON

WINSTER

6   5

TISSINGTON

ILAM   Thorpe Cloud ▲

ASHBOURNE

Relief of complete route

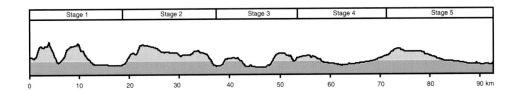

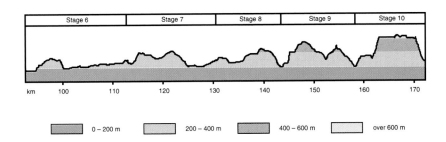

The walk is punctuated by 10 attractively located villages or hamlets that are linked by walking through most of the different types of Peak District scenery – including the rugged high edges, tors, ridges and moorlands around Kinder Scout and the Vale of Edale, together with the majority of the fascinating limestone dales further south. Through the White Peak the trek includes popular gorges and the lesser known valleys that connect them.

The starting locations were selected on the essential criterion that they offered adequate overnight accommodation over a wide price range (ideally from youth hostels to good, medium-sized hotels). Each location also had to provide several walking routes of varying severity, with maximum interest and variety along the way.

Finally, each stage had to have alternatives that could be completed within daylight hours, at most times of the year and in variable weather conditions, by walkers with widely different abilities and levels of fitness. This meant that each stage had to be well within a maximum distance of about 25 km (15 miles) and a total height climbed of under 1500 m (5000 ft), with easier short-cuts wherever feasible.

These constraints (especially those of overnight accommodation and all-weather walking) place the high-level moorlands surrounding Black Hill and Bleaklow out-of-bounds for this long-distance route. However, a taste of this wild, demanding terrain is afforded during the final stage of the walk, when the western edges of Kinder Scout are climbed and explored for some distance, *en route* from Hayfield to Edale. The extension suggested for this last stage crosses Kinder Plateau – a grand finale for any long-distance walk.

THE ROUTE

To cater for the needs of reasonably fit walkers, the main route is described in detail for each stage. It is envisaged that the majority of experienced walkers will follow the main route.

Edale is the suggested starting location, for two good reasons. Firstly, it is a popular tourist and walking centre with adequate accommodation in and around the village, and with good communication links, including a train service. Secondly Edale happens to be the official southern starting point of the Pennine Way and therefore the village caters for the needs of long-distance walkers. However, the walk may be commenced from any of the 10 suggested stopping places, most of which offer serious competition to Edale. The best starting location is probably the one that is most accessible for the individual walker.

Although the walk has been designed as a long-distance one to be completed within 10 days, there is no reason why the route cannot be undertaken over a considerably longer period of weeks, months or even years! Another approach is to tackle two or more stages over, say, a long weekend and to spend several weekends enjoyably completing the circuit. Some will no doubt jog all the way, aiming to reduce any existing record time for the route.

There are other options. For example, the complete route may be conveniently divided into two separate walks, each taking six days; a link of your own choosing between Baslow and Tideswell provides the necessary short-cut. There are also convenient opportunities to cut out individual stages at several points on the walk, thus reducing the time for the overall route to either nine or eight days.

Alternatives

For those who wish to tackle a more challenging itinerary, a number of optional extensions are provided for each stage whenever this is both feasible and sensible.

Easier alternatives are also provided for each stage and these are intended for those who might experience difficulties – which might include, for example, severely blistered toes or tummy trouble for a day or so. Temporary discomforts such as these need not jeopardize the completion of the entire circuit for those with a strict deadline. These suggested short-cuts might also be chosen when weather conditions deteriorate, a situation that can and should modify the most carefully conceived flexible plans for any challenging walk.

Route descriptions

The descriptive text for each stage is set out in an identical format and is illustrated by route diagrams and pertinent photographs.

An overview and statistics of the stage are summarized at the start of the chapter. These include a brief description of the starting location, details of public transport, a note on the landscape and features of interest, comments on footpaths and route finding, time allowances, the distance to be walked (including height), the overall height gained and the names and heights of the principal peaks visited. This is followed by a detailed descriptive text of the main route, and finally suggested variants.

TIME ALLOWANCES

The estimates of walking times allow for all stops, including lunch. They have been calculated on the basis of walking 4 km (2½ miles) in 1 hour, plus 1 hour for every 600 m (2000 ft) climbed and a further 1 hour for all stops. There is a final adjustment of up to plus or minus half an hour per stage to compensate for all other factors, such as difficulty of route finding, state of the paths, type of terrain, etc. You should adjust these basic estimates to suit your own pace.

ROUTE DIAGRAMS

The diagrams include a plan and an integrated cross-sectional relief that shows the profile of the walk. These diagrams are computer-generated and are based on the Ordnance Survey Outdoor Leisure Maps (OLMs) of the Peak District, scale 4 cm to 1 km (2½ inches to 1 mile) – the 1:25 000 series. The diagrams are therefore mathematically accurate in both plan and relief format, but they are not intended to substitute for a map when following the route.

PHOTOGRAPHS

The photographs are of two types: those taken when walking along the route, and those observing parts of the route from other vantage points. Camera symbols on the plan diagrams indicate the position and direction from which each photograph was taken. Each photograph is also identified by a number that appears next to the camera symbol in the plan diagram and also as part of the caption of the photograph, to facilitate cross-referencing. Each of these reference numbers has two components: the first part indicates the walking stage and the second the sequence of the photograph within each stage. For example: photograph 2:3 is the third sequential photograph taken during the second walking stage; 2:4 is the next in the sequence illustrating stage 2, and so on.

On average, each stage is illustrated by six colour photographs which are keyed into the walk, making them an additional aid to route finding. These photographs have been taken with a 35 mm Canon EOS 650 camera using a standard 50 mm lens, a 35–135 mm zoom lens and a polarizing filter. Fujichrome colour slide film has been used exclusively; on the later shots, the film of choice has been the improved Sensia 100 (which is now widely available).

OTHER CONSIDERATIONS

Other chapters in the book cover important considerations such as preparation, clothing, equipment, nourishment and safety, finding suitable overnight accommodation (there is a register of addresses) and comprehensive statistics of the walk.

Abbreviations

Abbreviations have been kept to a minimum and are used largely to avoid constant repetition of well-known compound words. They are listed in Table 1.

TABLE 1 **ABBREVIATIONS**

L	left	NW	north-west
R	right	NNW	north-north-west
N	north	cm	centimetre(s)
NNE	north-north-east	m	metre(s)
NE	north-east	km	kilometre(s)
ENE	east-north-east	ft	feet
E	east	K-gate	kissing-gate
ESE	east-south-east	G-stile	gap-stile
SE	south-east	L-stile	ladder-stile
SSE	south-south-east	P-stile	post-stile
S	south	S-stile	step-stile
SSW	south-south-west	W-stile	wall-stile
SW	south-west	MR	map reference
WSW	west-south-west	OLM	Outdoor Leisure Map
W	west	OS	Ordnance Survey
WNW	west-north-west	YH	Youth Hostel

Geological terms, dialect and place names

The geological terms, dialect words and place names used in the text are shown in Table 2.

TABLE 2 **GEOLOGICAL TERMS, DIALECT WORDS AND PLACE NAMES**

beck	stream
Blue John	variety of fluorite, containing purple, yellow or colourless bands
booth	herdsman's shelter or cow-shed
cairn	heap of stones, usually pointed
cavern	large natural space or chamber underground
clough	stream valley; narrow ravine
col	a sharp-edged or saddle-shaped pass
crag	steep, rugged rock or peak
culvert	drain or covered channel
dale	valley
edge	steep cliff
fault	a fracture in rocks the opposite sides of which have been displaced relative to one another, vertically or horizontally
ginnel	a narrow passageway between buildings
gorge	a deep, narrow, steep-walled valley
grit	coarse-grained, sandy sediment
grough/hag	a natural channel or fissure in a peat moor; a deep drainage ditch in a peat bog

Rock climbing above Froggatt

hause	summit of narrow pass; col
heath	large, open area with scrubby vegetation, usually comprising heathers
knoll	small, rounded hill
knott	rocky outcrop
limestone	a sedimentary rock composed almost entirely of calcium carbonate, mainly as calcite
millstone-grit	a coarse-grained carboniferous sandstone used for the manufacture of mill stones
nab/neb	promontory
pike	pointed summit
rindle	a stream which only flows in wet weather
rigg	ridge
sandstone	a sedimentary rock of sand and/or silt bound together by a cement, often calcite or silica; quartz grains predominate in the average sandstone
scar	escarpment
scree	loose shattered rock on mountain slope
shale	a fine-grained sedimentary rock formed predominantly of compacted clay
shippen	a cow-house
sinkhole	an area, especially in limestone, where a surface stream sinks underground
slough	a hole where water collects; a hollow filled with mud or bog
squeezer-stile	stile containing a narrow gap
toadstone	a Derbyshire name for decomposed basaltic volcanic rocks
tor	a core of unweathered harder rocks standing above a surrounding area of weathered rock
tower	tall, squarish structure of unweathered rock, usually located on or near the steep slopes of rocky gorges
well-dressing	custom of decorating wells with floral tributes in thanks for water

Lose Hill and far away Win Hill

Maps and compass

No guide-book is an adequate substitute for maps and a compass. At all times when you are walking around the Peak, use a reliable compass and the two Ordnance Survey Outdoor Leisure Maps 1 and 24, and Pathfinder Map 743 (Sheffield); scale 1:25 000. Be sure that you know how to use this combination correctly.

The Outdoor Leisure series is excellent and probably represents some of the finest mapping for walkers in the world. However, the maps are not infallible. In the rare instances where there are

differences in the route descriptions and the paths shown or not shown on the OLMs, rely on the route descriptions.

Harveys have extended considerably their 'Superwalker' range of waterproof 1:25 000 maps. When these practical and colourful maps become available for the whole of the Peak District, they will provide a viable alternative to the established OLM series; in wet weather they could become the maps of first choice.

COMPASS BEARINGS

All compass bearings have been given to the nearest 22½ degree point, e.g. N, NNE, NE, etc. This is considered to be sufficiently accurate over the relatively short distance between the taking of successive readings. Note that some rocks contain minerals with magnetic properties, so that certain compass bearings will not always be true. Therefore get into the habit of taking frequent confirmatory bearings when necessary, particularly when visibility is poor.

ARTIFICIAL FEATURES

Constructed features in the Peak District are constantly changing. Fences and walls appear and disappear, K-gates replace L-stiles and vice versa, additional waymarker signs materialize, other signs are removed, and so on. Should you spot isolated differences along the route from those described, presume that these have occurred since the book went to press and proceed with confidence to the next feature described. Care has been taken to include many references where you can be absolutely sure that you are standing at the right spot without being confused by these artificial features. Rely on these as your principal guide.

HILL HEIGHTS

The heights of the principal hills have been given in both metric and imperial measurements. The metric indicators are taken from the most up-to-date Ordnance Survey maps. Their imperial equivalents have been calculated by using a conversion factor of 0.3048 m = 1 ft. These equivalents have then been rounded off to the nearest 5 ft.

SPELLING

Sometimes there is more than one version of the spelling of place names. In such instances the spelling that appears on the OS OLMs has been used, unless otherwise indicated.

Morning stroll through Chatsworth Park

CONCEPT OF THE ROUTE AND USING THE BOOK

PREPARATION, GEAR
AND SAFETY

PREPARATION

The Peak District is not an inhospitable wilderness and the part chosen for this long-distance route is especially 'walker friendly'. Serious accidents to walkers within these hills and dales are extremely rare and, when they do occur, nearby mountain rescue teams are quickly on site. However, the moorlands and gorges demand respect and all walkers who venture into this exciting terrain should be properly equipped and well versed in rudimentary mountain-craft.

The circuit has been conceived as an all-weather route suitable for most walkers who are reasonably fit. They are strongly advised to prepare themselves and gain adequate experience by first completing at least two or three consecutive full days of walking over the type of landscape that they will encounter in The Peaks – a combination of exposed hilly terrain and sheltered dales. This apprenticeship provides practical experience of what clothing, equipment and nourishment should be taken and what sensible safety precautions are needed on this type of expedition.

Mountain-craft

It is essential that all groups of walkers who undertake this long-distance walk should include members who are proficient in navigation, are able to interpret and anticipate changing weather patterns in hilly terrain, and are competent in administering basic first aid. They must also be able to cope with accidents and illnesses, including mountain rescue procedures. Only strong and very experienced walkers should attempt the route in winter and in such conditions all members of the party should have received adequate training in snow and ice techniques; they should know how to maintain security in a potentially hostile environment, even though deep, lying snow is uncommon in these parts. The leader should continuously ensure that members of the party do not become separated.

First aid

A snow-capped Kinder Scout

With knowledge of basic first aid techniques and the application of common sense, an expert and well-equipped walking party ought to deal competently with most of the injuries that might occur during the walk. The primary purposes of administering first aid are to reassure, comfort and keep warm an injured person, and to relieve any life-threatening condition.

All leaders of walking groups – and preferably all walkers – should attend recognized first aid courses conducted under the auspices of St John Ambulance, the British Red Cross or similar bodies. All participants should be proficient in coping by modern methods with emergencies such as absence of breath or pulse, clearing an obstructed airway, arresting severe bleeding, protecting an injured companion and safely removing a victim from any life-threatening hazard. A recognized guide-book to mountaineering first aid should be studied by all those venturing into these high places.

TABLE 3 **FIRST AID KIT**

All seasons

Assorted plasters and strip	Insect repellent
Dumb-bell sutures	Surgical spirit
Bandages, including:	Cotton wool pads
triangular	Ibuprofen
elastic (for sprains)	Scissors
Wound dressing	Safety pins
Chiropody felt	Luggage labels
Antiseptic wipes	

Weather

It is important to recognise that English weather is very fickle at *all* times of the year. Conditions can change rapidly – sometimes with almost frightening speed, particularly in hilly regions.

Also our weather has a habit of not heeding the seasons. You might be basking in shirt-sleeves during February, or battling in your storm-gear through mid-summer gales with lashing rain and winter-like wind-chill factors. No matter how pleasant the weather is at the start, always anticipate that weather conditions could change significantly during the several days of your walk.

CLOTHING, EQUIPMENT AND NOURISHMENT

Comprehensive lists of the items I would consider taking with me on this route are provided in Tables 3, 4 , 5 and 6. Some of the items might seem obvious but these tables serve as useful checklists – the most basic and essential items are often overlooked! My final selection depends upon a judgement about likely weather conditions but I always take a woollen ski hat, thin woollen gloves or mitts and a torch, irrespective of the time of year, or of the weather conditions at the start. I never carry a towel, as these are usually provided by bed-and-breakfast establishments.

You will no doubt add some of your own preferences to the list but do bear in mind overall weight constraints. Take sufficient quantities of each item only to last just beyond the intended duration of your walk. Where possible, share items such as washing powder with your companions.

Weight constraints

On no account burden yourself with a load so heavy and cumbersome that it detracts from your enjoyment of the walk. An unwieldy load also causes unnecessary fatigue which could result in an avoidable accident.

There are practical limits as to the weight and size of the burden that you can reasonably carry over so many kilometres of demanding, hilly terrain. Depending on physique, sensible weight limits for filled ruck-sacks are about 10 kg (25 lb) for men and perhaps 2 kg (about 5 lb) less for women. Further weight is added by carrying a camera, binoculars and, when necessary, an ice axe and crampons. Before tackling the full route, it would be sensible to test the weight of your load by practising with a similar one for at least two full days consecutively.

A heavy load will anyway feel uncomfortable for the first day or two until you have become more accustomed to its bulk. During this familiarization period be particularly careful to prevent the straps of your rucksack from chafing your shoulders, or the frame from rubbing against your hips. To minimize such risks, take some of the natural strain off your upper back and other normal pressure points from time to time by placing your thumbs through the shoulder straps and distributing part of the weight to your hands and arms, alternating this with cupping your hands and forearms beneath the rucksack and pushing gently upwards to distribute the load further.

TABLE 4 **EQUIPMENT**

All seasons

Money and cheque book (incl. coins for phone)	Thermos flask
Credit cards	Water bottle
Stamps and postcards	Food container
Identification	Survival bag
Wallet	Notebook and pen
Rucksack	Camera and lenses
Waterproof liner	Films
Maps	Spare camera batteries
Compass	Binoculars
Watch	String
Guide book	Needle and thread
Head-torch	Spare buttons
Spare bulb and batteries	Toilet paper
Whistle	Toiletries
Swiss Army knife	Washing-up powder

Extras for hot summer weather

Sunglasses	Sun-cream and lip salve

Extras for extreme winter weather

Ski goggles	Crampons
Ice axe	

Clothing

Obviously the time of year and the prevailing weather conditions will determine what clothes you wear and carry. In all but cold, wet, windy weather, I have found that the dominant problem is one of avoiding excessive perspiration when on the move and I now pace myself accordingly. However, when you stop for longer than a moment, immediately put on extra warm clothing – do not wait until you feel chilled!

Good quality waterproof outer garments and a warm sweater or fleece jacket are essential and there is a variety of reliable makes. My own preference is the excellent Sprayway range, in particular their 'Torridon' Goretex jacket and their 'Enigma' fleece. Sprayway also do colourful, warm head-gear that is perfect for cold winter days.

On no account should denim jeans be worn. They can become extremely uncomfortable when wet and in such conditions the loss of body heat through them is considerable, significantly increasing the risk of hypothermia.

Robust boots that provide adequate waterproof protection are essential, but they should be comfortable and well 'worn in'. There is a wide choice. Boots that have constantly satisfied my own demands are the Raichle 'Zermatt' and 'Sporty 2' models, and Brasher's 'Hill Master'. My choice from these three excellent and reliable boots would depend upon the time of year and the most likely weather pattern during the walk.

Frosty morning at Baslow

TABLE 5 **CLOTHING**

Normal weather

Breathable waterproofs	2 changes of underwear
Ultra-fleece jacket	2 changes of socks
Breeches	2 extra shirts
Woollen ski hat or balaclava	Clothes for evenings
Fine woollen mitts	Handkerchiefs
Thermal underwear	Spare bootlaces

Extras for hot summer weather

Shorts	Sun-hat

Extras for extreme winter weather

Additional sweater	Thermal ski mitts
Storm gear	Waterproof gaiters

Nutrition

Always take more than adequate food and drink with you, to cope with unexpected emergencies, and try to conserve a small amount of this until your final destination is in sight. Concentrates such as glucose tablets, chocolate, nuts, raisins and boiled sweets take up very little room in proportion to their energy content. Liquid refreshment can usually be supplemented from natural resources such as fast-flowing streams – but only as a fall-back and then only consume minimum quantities of untreated water.

TABLE 6 **NOURISHMENT**

Normal weather

Food	Chocolate
Drink	Boiled sweets
Glucose tablets	

Extras for hot summer weather

Additional cold drink

Extras for extreme winter weather

Additional hot drink	Emergency rations

SAFETY

Safety precautions are aimed at cutting down risk to an absolute acceptable minimum. To start with, only venture on to exposed high moorlands and up craggy tors well prepared, carrying detailed maps of the area, a reliable compass, a torch, an adequate first aid kit and a reserve of food and drink. Be appropriately clothed and take with you additional protective apparel. These items will make a significant contribution to the prevention of accidents and to avoiding other unfortunate incidents. Additionally, before you set out, carefully conceive a clear but flexible route plan.

Each morning, give details of your planned route to the proprietors of the place where you have stayed overnight and also to those at the next intended port of call (if this has been decided).

Along the way make a practice of taking frequent compass bearings, particularly in misty conditions. Always know where you are within short distances: learn to recognize distinctive landmarks that will pinpoint your location in relation to grid coordinates on the map. Until you reach the next easily recognizable location, ensure that you can always retrace your steps to the last certainly identified position without undue difficulty. Know when to curtail your intended route if this becomes necessary because of appalling weather conditions.

The most important common-sense precaution is to watch where you are putting your feet! In some situations this can be critical. For example, when walking across a rock-fall or descending a steep, slippery slope, it is essential to concentrate fully on this simple discipline. When scrambling over craggy outcrops, always test that critical hand-holds will momentarily bear your full weight – just in case.

Illness and serious accidents

In the event of serious injury from, say, a fall or being hit by dislodged rock, the first rule is to think before you act. *Do not move the casualty* unless the victim is in imminent danger, in which case do not move them more than is absolutely necessary for their immediate safety – for example, if they are in the path of imminent further rock or snow and ice falls – until the full extent of injury has been competently diagnosed. This is especially important if there is suspected injury to the spine, head or neck, when, if the need to move is unquestionable, a scoop stretcher or similar equipment must be used. This, however, should not be attempted without proper medical training. In other cases, a person can be dragged a short distance if necessary by grasping the clothing near the shoulders, the head supported on the rescuer's

The RAF to the rescue at Ashway Rocks

forearms, and then pulling him/her along gently and uniformly in a straight line.

If an incapacitating illness or accident renders further progress by a member of the group either impossible or extremely difficult, the prime task is to summon expert help from a mountain rescue team as quickly as possible. Before you do so, give any essential first aid and make your companion as comfortable and as warm as possible. With any injured person, the prevention of wind chill is an important consideration and it is imperative to move that person (or a hypothermic casualty) into shelter protected from the wind.

If there are more than two in the party, decide who is going to remain with the injured person and who is going to summon help. Before leaving, place as much food and drink within easy reach of the victim as you can and firmly attach an accident report to the person, giving details of the injury or illness, the time this occurred, first aid rendered, and where you are making for and to what purpose. Do this even if the injured person is fully conscious at the time of your departure and irrespective of whether members of your party remain with the victim. Evacuate all members of the group who are not needed either to go for help or to stay and attend to the needs of the casualty.

With a larger party, and whenever possible, at least two members should go for help. In as composed a frame of mind as possible, they should take an exact map reference of the spot, memorize the distinctive land features there, note the time and make fast but controlled progress to the nearest farm, hamlet or road with the objective of reaching a phone in order to dial the emergency services via the police on 999.

If you meet fellow walkers during this quest, alert them to your predicament and ask them either to locate your stricken companion or to accompany you in search of expert help. On no account delegate to anybody else the most important part of your present mission, i.e. that of summoning professional assistance. *Always do this yourself*, including making the critical contact telephone call. Your companion's life might rest on this and it is far too important a matter to trust to others.

Be aware of the emergency signal when in the hills. This is six short blasts on a whistle, or flashes with a torch, repeated at intervals of one minute. The answering acknowledgement is three such blasts or flashes.

Looking after your feet

Most walkers will be lucky if they manage to avoid relatively minor problems with their feet during this exacting 10-day walk. However, take sensible precautions to prevent any really painful blistering or broken skin on the toes or around the heel. First of all, only use boots that are comfortable and well worn in. The best sock combination, I find, is a thin inner pair of 100 per cent soft wool, and a thicker, padded, more robust outer pair. (Other walkers prefer to wear one pair of thick, loop-stitch stockings.) Try to rinse out your inner socks each evening.

The only foot problem I have experienced on long-distance walks is that, after a few days, sore and tender spots occasionally appear on my toes but fortunately with no broken skin. If this occurs, it can usually be controlled by dabbing the offending spots with surgical spirit. Never attempt to use this remedy on raw flesh!

Overleaf: Above Dove Dale

Stage 1

EDALE TO
HATHERSAGE

1 Looking down on Edale Village

Stage 1: EDALE to HATHERSAGE

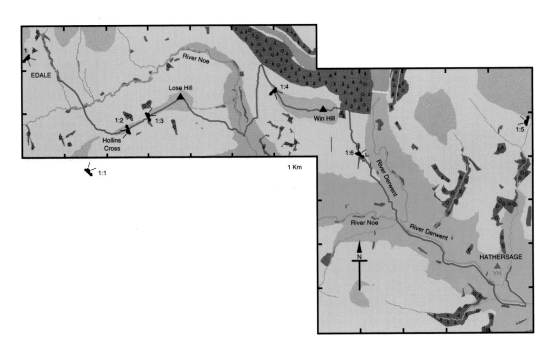

EDALE
River Noe
Lose Hill
1:2
1:3
Hollins
Cross
1:1
Win Hill
1:4
1:5
1:6
River Derwent
River Noe
River Derwent
HATHERSAGE
YH
N
1 Km

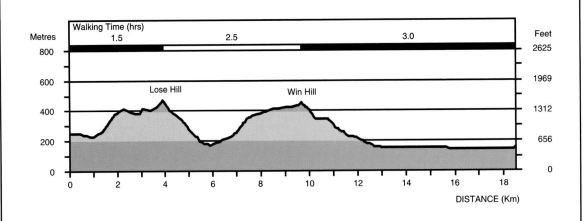

Walking Time (hrs)		
1.5	2.5	3.0

Metres — Feet

800 — 2625
600 — 1969
400 — 1312
200 — 656
0 — 0

Lose Hill
Win Hill

DISTANCE (Km)
0 2 4 6 8 10 12 14 16 18

STARTING LOCATION

Edale Village in the Vale of Edale just below Grindsbrook Clough. Reached by minor loop road off A625.

OLM 1/MR 123860 (also use Pathfinder Map 743, Sheffield).

Large car and coach parking facilities and toilets near railway station to S of village.

Directions start from the top end of the village outside the Old Nag's Head Inn.

PUBLIC TRANSPORT

Bus routes 260 (Edale, Castleton)and 403 (Crystal Peaks, Chesterfield, Edale, Hayfield).

Train service (Sheffield, Hope Valley, Manchester).

OVERVIEW/INTEREST

Attractive village of Edale with National Park Information Centre.

Superb ridge walk amongst wide open spaces.

Interesting weathered tors of Lose Hill and Win Hill.

Secluded section along placid River Derwent.

Panoramic views of Kinder, Edale and Hope Valleys and Ladybower Reservoir.

FOOTPATHS/WAYSIGNS

Footpaths, with few exceptions, good to excellent.

Virtual absence of waterlogged ground.

Some erosion still to be sorted out along ridgeways and by the banks of the River Derwent (spring 1995).

Route fairly obvious and adequate signs in position where most needed.

Walking through Thornhill a bit complicated but no significant challenges.

OVERALL TIME ALLOWANCE 7 hours

Statistics		
Distance walked	**Km**	**Miles**
	18.6	11.5
Height climbed	**M**	**Feet**
	590	1935
Principal heights	**M**	**Feet**
Lose Hill	476	1560
Win Hill	462	1515

The Way to Lose Hill (Allow 1½ hours)

The walk starts from the Old Nag's Head Inn. This also happens to be the starting point of the long-distance Pennine Way, which tracks northwards across some really challenging terrain, finishing up about 400 km (250 miles) away in Scotland. Your own route is a less demanding circular one to the south, finishing back at the Nag's Head after a 160-km (100-mile) trek.

From the Nag's Head, walk down the lane that leads S through the elongated village to reach the church of the Holy and Undivided Trinity. (This is just before reaching the National Park Visitor Centre, which is well worth visiting.) Opposite the church entrance, turn L over a stile and climb down the steps leading to the stream (Grinds Brook). The way crosses the brook. After a G-stile, turn R down the footpath signed to 'Castleton via Hollins Cross', and continue SE. After a squeeze through a second narrow G-stile, pass a barn to your R. The road through the Vale of Edale is then approached on a diagonal which involves using a tunnel beneath the railway line and then veering L to follow the way indicated by a footpath sign and a yellow arrowhead marker. Beyond the next G-stile, steer R beside the stone wall and walk down to the road. This is reached at MR 129853. Spacious views immediately appear along this initial section of the walk and in clear weather the continuation route up to and along the fine ridge leading towards Lose Hill presents exciting prospects. To your rear, beyond the flatness and neatness of Edale Valley (as the Vale of Edale is known locally), the plateau of Kinder Scout soars to a height of some 600 m (2000 ft). Part of the SW edges of this plateau will provide your return route into Edale on another day.

Cross the road and the River Noe, negotiating more stiles in so doing. Continue up the footpath ahead, again signed to 'Hollins Cross and Castleton'. Deviate to the R when you reach a line of hawthorn trees (this is before Hollins Farm, which you bypass to the R). The way is then more directly uphill on a SSE heading. A short distance further on, a flight of stone steps will lead you to a gap in an obstructing stone wall. Beyond these minor obstacles an obvious, eroded path tracks diagonally SE to the crest of the undulating ridge linking Mam Tor with Lose Hill. This is reached at Hollins Cross (MR 136845). A large stone memorial dedicated to Tom Hyett of Long Eaton, a respected former member of the Ramblers' Association, marks the spot. There

1:1 *The ridge linking Mam Tor and Lose Hill*

are new vistas of the extensive lower ground forming Hope Valley and of the collapsed road over the shivering slopes of Mam Tor with its unstable bedding planes of grits and shales. The village of Castleton lies snugly below to the SE and the buildings of Hope are discernible in clear weather further away to the E down the wooded valley.

Veer L along the undulating ridge to continue due E. The way across the chain of hillocks narrows and becomes increasingly spectacular as you approach the crumbling, craggy shape of Back Tor that soon rears up ahead. When approaching this hill, pass over the second of two stiles to cross a wire fence to your L at a point signed to 'Back Tor and Lose Hill'. The rocky landscape directly ahead becomes quite rugged but the otherwise harshness of this spot is softened by a small cluster of Scots pines. These trees are the only remnants of an extensive forest that once covered these exposed slopes. A short, sharp, steeper slope leads up rougher, rocky ground to the top of the tor where the best views are near the crumbling NW edge. Exercise care in approaching this face of Back Tor, particularly in gusty wind or icy conditions.

Broad grassy slopes lead further eastwards from Back Tor, first down to a shallow col and then up again to the higher peak of Lose Hill, alternatively named 'Ward's Piece' on the OLM. This summit commands a height of 476 m (1560 ft) and it forms the easterly extremity of the ridge. The rounded top provides a superb viewing platform in clear weather. Within the extensive landscapes visible

1:2 *Hollins Cross (Mam Tor ridge)*

from here, the continuation route as far as the tor of Win Hill (shaped like a wedge of cheese from this viewpoint) is revealed. This lies just over 3 km (about 2 miles) further E, although your walking distance to get there is appreciably more than this. The positions of many of the other impressive sightings from this peak have been previously mentioned but the correct direction of these and others are indicated on a fine illustrated compass seated on the top of a substantial circular mound built on this summit.

The way to Win Hill *(Allow 2½ hours)*

Commence your descent along the obvious path dropping to the SE. The pleasant way down curves first R and then L as it hugs the contortions of the ridge. The first section is relatively steep along a partially renovated way and this can become tricky in icy conditions. The gradient eases as you approach a fence running at right angles and which you cross at a stile. Rounded, grassy slopes lie ahead. Immediately past the fence, bear L at a junction of ways to continue down the crest of the ridge as it bends round more directly in line with Win Hill away to the E. A pleasant descent down springy, grassy slopes is briefly interrupted by an awkward angled stile.

Another stile in a more enclosed setting has to be negotiated before a tree-lined, shallow gully is entered and through which the now stony path continues to descend. The gully terminates at another stile. Over this, turn L to follow a wider macadam track which winds down to the minor road through the Vale of Edale below. This road is reached near Underleigh Country House at MR 168845. Turn L along the Edale Road to cross, almost immediately, the River Noe by means of the ancient stone bridge (Townhead Bridge). Then keep walking straight ahead, abandoning the road as it turns L, to continue northwards along a walled track and passing by a stone barn to your R. The correct way is signed 'Footpath to Open Country' and from here the route winds gently uphill beneath trees. Through gaps in the foliage there are interesting views back towards Lose Hill on your L.

Higher up there are wide views of the lower slopes leading to Win Hill. These are ablaze with purple hues in late August and early September when the vast areas of heather are in bloom. The railway line is crossed by passing under Bridge 39. After this, always keep to the obvious main track as it continues to gain height at a comfortable rate and follow this round as it swings abruptly L, towards N, at Fullwood Stile Farm. Keep bearing L ahead, ignoring a branch path off to the R that leads to a gate. Height continues to be gained along a rougher track which continues along a shallow cleft as another side

1:3 *A snow-covered approach to Lose Hill*

track off to the R is passed, before a turning area for sheep trailers at The Brinks is reached. Keep to your established upwards diagonal beyond this. After passing through a metal gate, bear R along the higher path which immediately leads out on to the open, bracken-covered hillside along a rough path, initially stony. This soon gives way to a more comfortable grassy route.

An obvious wide, terraced way then leads further up the hillside affording splendid views down into the wooded Edale Valley with the pointed shape of Lose Hill dominating its eastern extremity. After a steeper section, the way up flattens off in the vicinity of a prominent rectangular stone pillar, presumably the remains of a former gateway.

The grass slopes hereabouts are a real joy to tread over. Beyond this landmark, the main ridge is quite quickly reached near a dense plantation of Scots pine towards which your approach path leads directly. However, do not go as far as these trees; instead turn full R along the clear ridge path, almost immediately passing another redundant stone column as your way seeks out still higher grounds. The important turning to the R is at MR 172861 and this changes your direction of travel to SSE.

1:4 The heather-clad slopes leading to Win Hill

A delightful open stretch now follows to reach the summit of Win Hill, also named Winhill Pike on the OLM, less than 2 km (1¼ miles) further on at the easterly end of the rising spur. Magnificent views in all directions abound in favourable weather and to your rear there is a particularly revealing view to the NW of the greater part of Jaggers Clough tearing into the side of Crookstone Out Moor on the far eastern slopes of Kinder Plateau. Ahead is your next major objective: the irregular jumble of rocks forming the summit of Win Hill, which you approach along an agreeable ridge path. Always keep to the apex of the ridge in this approach, avoiding all paths on either side.

At the top of an intervening rise, look to your L to see the impressive, arched concrete bridge carrying the main A57 road across Ladybower Reservoir. Only the top-most section of this bridge protrudes above the water. Your route then bisects another path connecting the Ladybower Reservoir to the N with Hope village. This is near Thornhill Brink at MR 183851. A short distance further on is the outcrop of harder rocks and boulders that form the summit cone

1:5 *A distant view of the descent ridge from Win Hill*

of Win Hill. The path up these is round to the R in the lee of the tor, unless you fancy a more challenging scramble of your own choosing up through the large jumble of boulders directly ahead that mark the apex of the exposed summit wedge. Be careful if you attempt this.

By means of either approach route, make your way to the trig point at the top of Win Hill, standing at 462 m (1515 ft), to be rewarded by more extensive revelations of the Ladybower and Derwent Reservoir system backed by the wild landscapes of Howden and Derwent Moors. Stretching away to the E are the long, gritty profiles and boulder-strewn slopes of Bamford Edge. Above this, Stanage Edge contains plenty of challenging, shorter climbing routes. Some of the familiar views to the W will disappear as you start your descent from Win Hill.

The way to Hathersage *(Allow 3 hours)*

Leave the summit along the path which leads down NE, initially along a narrow, rocky, elevated spur. The route then traverses wider slopes which extend in the direction of Bamford Edge on the far side of the valley further to the E. The ground remains rough and the steep path down is rocky with a surface of loose debris that demands the exercise of continuous care to avoid the possibility of a twisted ankle. This caution also applies to the crossing of a high stile part way down which has particularly wide steps, at the top of which you are advised to turn about to descend in safety. After this, the going improves along a more grassy section but this is only a temporary respite as there is still some harsh ground to be crossed.

Entering the scattered woodlands of Winhill Plantation, mainly of larch to your L and a mixture of deciduous trees including beech, oak and sycamore to your R, signals that the worst of the descent is over. Turn R along a wide path when you reach a wire fence, thus abandoning the steep continuation way down into the valley through a stile to your L. The R turn is at MR 192851. Now you should be walking due S along a pleasant, grassy path which leads gently uphill between heathers along a shallow depression. The sward then traverses round the flank of the hillside, maintaining a fairly constant height. There are extensive views down into the steep-sided valley of the River Derwent to your L, where the buildings of the oblong village of Bamford are clearly visible. Further away to the SE are the wider, lower reaches of the Hope Valley.

At Thornhill Carrs, a short distance further on, another path is bisected. At this juncture bear L downhill along the main grassy path, avoiding a side path through a gap in the stone walling which leads towards Aston. Descend along your selected path SSE towards the village of Thornhill but be constantly mindful of the extremely steep and unexpected fall-away down to your L. The way leads through clumps

1:6 *Looking back towards Ladybower Reservoir*

of gorse, after which be vigilant to locate and follow a narrow side path that leads down more steeply to the L to bring you to a wooden stile directly below. The route continues to drop down the hillside maintaining a SSE diagonal and beyond a wooden gate the way is often a wee bit muddy. Through the worst of these waterlogged areas, the way continues to descend through a belt of trees and further on a gate and narrow G-stile provide an entrance to more enclosed terrain where encroaching foliage quite often needs to be pushed away as you continue along a narrowing path.

The way then leads to a group of houses and these signal that you are entering the tiny village of Thornhill. On your approach to these houses, ignore the side path through stone pillars off to your L and continue instead along the macadam minor lane, walking SSW. This is Town Head Lane. Next, veer L round Ryecroft Farm to proceed SE down a narrow, banked lane where a small chapel is passed to your R. This lane leads down to a T-junction at Carr Lane (MR 199834) where you turn R in the direction signed to 'Bamford 2 Hope 2½'. After about 50 paces, be careful to locate and turn L along a narrow path, accessed by means of a stile, which leads gently further downhill SE towards the Hope Valley. A second stile then provides an entrance to a wider path along which you bear R, still walking slightly downhill.

Lower down, turn L along a concession bridleway and then turn R over a stile opposite the Quaker Community Buildings to continue along a footpath which hugs the edge of the adjacent field. The way then bends to the R before it sweeps round to the L to continue adjacent to the railway line. Over another stile, turn sharp R to pass beneath the railway line. Beyond a gate ahead, pass an extensive nursery to your L before crossing the main A625 road at MR 203826. A K-gate provides access to this crossing but be careful to walk L away from the dangerous bend before passing over the busy road. Almost immediately, cross the River Noe by means of a stone bridge, then turn L to pass through a G-stile and follow the public footpath signed to 'Leadmill'.

The way then crosses a tributary stream. On the far side, turn L and then veer L again at the next fork to continue walking SE along the course of the main stream which now contains the catchment waters of both the River Noe and the larger River Derwent beyond their confluence at MR 205825. There is a delightful stretch from here of some 4 km (2½ miles) along the wooded banks of the placid River Derwent. There are one or two steep drops down to the L and one spot (spring 1995) is quite slippery. Make use of a succession of stiles, wooden gates and bridges across side streams as you progress through a landscape of gullies and broad, flat meadowlands during your undemanding approach to Leadmill Bridge. There is one simple rule along here: do not stray far from the banks of the river over on your L. Where choices of way appear, always select the L-hand one which will lead you closest to the river. In particular, avoid a public footpath to the R signed to 'Offerton'.

The riverside path eventually leads you to the B6001 road at Leadmill Bridge, reached through two more stiles. Turn L to cross over the River Derwent by means of the arched bridge, then turn off the road almost immediately along the next footpath on your L through a K-gate. This path leads along a NW diagonal into the outskirts of Hathersage, your final walking destination for the day. During the approach to the village, bear L along a lane at the end of the pathway and this will lead you beneath a railway viaduct into the centre of the village to complete the first stage of the walk.

Alternatives

EXTENSIONS

This is already a fairly demanding introductory stage to the long-distance walk and, assuming you are undertaking the complete walk in one go, you will almost certainly be carrying a rucksack about twice as heavy as that you would normally be transporting on a single day out in the hills. Therefore, no extensions are recommended to the main route described.

A more rugged route from Edale to Win Hill is to climb up to Ringing Roger on the rim of Kinder Plateau above Edale and then to use the rocky indent of Jaggers Clough to reach the systems of footpaths leading eastwards to Hope Cross. From the cross, a good path leads SE along the rising ridge above the forestry plantations lining the Woodlands Valley and this connects with the main route at MR 172861.

EASIER ROUTES

It is possible to avoid climbing Lose Hill by using a combination of the valley paths and road along Edale. This lower route is via Ollerbrook Booth and through the grounds of the Youth Hostel near Rowland Cote. However, this is not recommended for several reasons – including the fact that the route is complicated, height is avoided only at the expense of a greater ground distance and you will miss the splendid views that can be observed from the higher ground .

A more practical possibility is to leave out Win Hill. To avoid this second climb, when you have descended from Lose Hill to Edale Road bear right down the road and follow this into the village of Hope. Continue S from here to connect with the footpaths running W to E along Hope Valley S of the River Noe. These are reached at MR 172832. Turn L to walk eastwards along these through Brough and then along Townfield Lane, round Wheat Hay Farm, to rejoin the main route at MR 203826.

Stage 2

HATHERSAGE TO BASLOW

2 Callow Bank and Higger Tor

Stage 2: HATHERSAGE to BASLOW

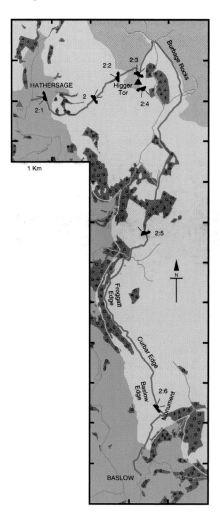

1 Km

Burbage Rocks

HATHERSAGE

YH

2:1

2

2:2

Higger
Tor

2:3

2:4

2:5

N

Froggatt
Edge

Curbar Edge

Baslow
Edge

2:6

Monument

BASLOW

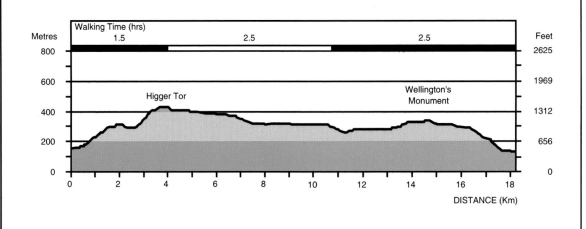

Metres	Walking Time (hrs)			Feet
	1.5	2.5	2.5	
800				2625
600				1969
	Higger Tor		Wellington's Monument	1312
400				
200				656
0				0

0   2   4   6   8   10   12   14   16   18

DISTANCE (Km)

STARTING LOCATION

Hathersage Village situated at the junction of the A625 and B6001 roads a short distance W of the outskirts of Sheffield.

Pathfinder Map 743 (Sheffield)/MR 230815 (also use OLM 24).

Directions start from the centre of the village at the road junction.

PUBLIC TRANSPORT

Served by many local and mainline bus routes including 174, 254, 257, 272, 276, 280, 309, 403 and 796. These (in the order the routes are cited) link Castleton, Bakewell, Ilkeston, Matlock, Sheffield, Derwent, Chesterfield, Buxton, Calver, Crystal Peaks, Edale and Hayfield.

Train service (Sheffield, Hope Valley, Manchester).

OVERVIEW/INTEREST

Variety of scenery from enclosed woodlands to wide open spaces.

Delights of boulder-strewn Higger Tor and Burbage Rocks.

Route passes through Longshaw Country Park.

Succession of gritstone edges including those of Froggatt, Curbar and Baslow.

Eagle Stone and Wellington's Monument visited.

Magnificent views throughout.

FOOTPATHS/WAYSIGNS

Footpaths are fairly obvious and no significant route-finding difficulties should be experienced.

The going is nearly always firm and the paths and sightseeing diversions along the extended Edges are really delightful.

Virtually no waterlogged ground.

Signs are adequate but far from numerous.

OVERALL TIME ALLOWANCE 6½ hours

Statistics		
Distance walked	**Km**	**Miles**
	18.5	11.5
Height climbed	**M**	**Feet**
	390	1280
Principal heights	**M**	**Feet**
Higger Tor	434	1425
Highest point along Edges	340	1115

The way to Higger Tor *(Allow 1½ hours)*

From the centre of the village of Hathersage at the junction of the A625 and B6001 roads, set off E along the A625 road walking uphill in the direction of Sheffield. The escape from the confines of the village leads past the Hathersage Inn and 'Outside', a well-stocked shop for outdoor leisure clothing and equipment. Keep walking along the main road for just under 1 km (about ½ mile) passing by Hall Farm and School Lane, using the pavement on alternate sides of the road wherever possible. As height is progressively gained, the first glimpses appear of the extensive gritstone edges rising to the E. There are also revealing views to your rear of the green hilly countryside surrounding Hathersage, the buildings of which sprawl up the nearest slopes.

Be careful to locate and take a signed public footpath to your L which commences up a macadam track adjacent to a building that

houses a distinctive weather vane. Your new direction is to the SE as the track leads further uphill to the rear of several dwellings on your R. The smooth, surfaced track soon gives way to a wide gravel way which winds uphill through a small strip of deciduous woodland. Beyond a wooden fence containing a rickety access gate, the narrow path (now composed of compacted earth) allows you to gain further height under a canopy of beech, sweet chestnut and sycamore trees and further on beneath pine trees. Higher up still the trunk of a tree, fallen long ago, has to be ducked under. The steepness of the gradient abates hereabouts.

The route then reaches the corner of a stone wall near a gate bearing the word 'Private'. Veer L here to follow the continuation path beside the stone wall, now adjacent on your R. Two S-stiles are crossed and the second of these allows access to wilder, bracken-covered countryside. From here a wide, grassy path leads to a junction of ways at MR 243813. Turn L to walk NE towards the renovated buildings of Scraperlow with their central castellated parapet. These buildings are passed on your L as you veer R round the boundary wall. Further on, bear R again to continue along a narrowing peaty path through bracken and across stretches that hold surface water following heavy rain. The continuation way ENE is signed 'Public Footpath to Mitchell Field Farm'. Along here there are views of the higher ground of Burbage Rocks away to the E. In an area now encompassing expansive moorlands topped by pointed tors and long gritstone edges, part of the long escarpment of Stanage Edge appears to the N, terminating at the Cowper Stone above White Path Moss. The panorama is superb in fine weather. To the NE you will see the rocky outcrops of Callow Bank and Higger Tor.

Eventually an S-stile breaches a stone wall ahead and this, in autumn 1994, was badly in need of some urgent repair. The stile provides entry into the Mitchell Field Farm Conservation area and sensible restrictions are placed upon your passage through this field centre. Cross the adjacent field on a short diagonal to your L to clamber over another stone wall by means of an awkwardly positioned S-stile and wooden barrier. After this second obstacle, a narrow path leads down to a surfaced private drive a short distance ahead, along which you are permitted to walk. Turn L and use the driveway to skirt round the buildings on your L, avoiding a footpath leading off on the R. Then pass through a wooden gate before bearing R along a grassy track and bypassing a narrower path leading down to your L.

Next, pass over another S-stile adjacent to a metal gate, turn full R at the T-junction ahead and continue uphill along the signed footpath, now making progress to the ESE up a wide, walled track. Turn off the track to cross a wire fence to your L by means of a wooden S-stile. A rougher path leads further uphill from here towards the edges above. The path eventually flattens off and beyond a short stretch covered in heather it converges on the minor road linking Hathersage Booths with Upper Burbage Bridge. This is at MR 256823. Cross the road, climb the steps ahead and you will be standing on the top of Higger Tor at a height of 434 m (1425 ft).

2:2 *The westwards vista down along Hope Valley*

The views from this exposed jumble of rocks and boulders are out-standing in favourable weather and the extensive upthrust area deserves some detailed exploration. The major landscapes to be admired from here include: to the N and E the massive U-shaped edges of Fiddler's Elbow and Burbage Rocks with their apex centred around Upper Burbage Bridge in the N and cupping delightful, forested areas below; to the S the receding hills and spurs falling towards the flat, orderly parklands of Chatsworth; to the W the rounded hills over which you have just walked from Hathersage with the Hope Valley stretching further away beyond these; and to the R and above the Hope Valley, the twin pointed peaks of Lose Hill and Win Hill with the higher ground of Kinder Plateau providing the backcloth.

2:3 *Walkers approaching Higger Tor*

One other delight up here is that this tor is a favourite visiting spot for families living in the Sheffield area. Conversations with the adventurous youngsters, who more often than not beat their accompanying adults to the top, are a reminder that the precious National Parks justify all that is wisely being invested in them for the sake of future generations.

The way to the Grouse Inn *(Allow 2½ hours)*

Descend from Higger Tor along the waymarked sandy path that leads northwards along the escarpment named Fiddler's Elbow. This is a good, invariably dry section of the route through a mixture of bracken and heather along a rocky edge. Following the initial drop, the path maintains a more or less constant height that permits fast progress. Further on, bear R up an outcrop of boulders. Beyond this, the now more peaty path leads back towards the minor road but, before reaching the road, turn R to cross the stream (Burbage Brook) by means of stepping slabs below the arched road bridge. This adventurous crossing is at MR 261830. Continue along the signed public footpath which leads SSE below the vertical face of Burbage Rocks. These rocks are famous for their short climbing pitches and there are countless recognized routes, varying widely in severity. There are further superb views from here southwards down the forested valley to Higger Tor and further on the outcrop of Carl Wark (evidence of ancient Iron Age settlement), dominating the hillsides that shield the western flank of the valley.

2:4 *The southerly panorama from the rocks of Higger Tor*

A good, wide, sandy way winds SSE just below the edges and the relative security of footing along here affords you the opportunity to look up and admire the technique of climbers testing their skills on the intermingled jumble of loose rocks and boulders and firm rock buttresses. Your way leads generally southwards in a gradual curve to the R and along here there is an interesting up-welling of water adjacent to the footpath. Always keep to the main footpath, particularly as it descends towards the road ahead and where there are inviting paths leading off to both sides. After passing through a couple of gates and stiles, the road (the A625) is reached at the National Trust property at Longshaw, MR 263806.

Pass through a K-gate on the far side of the road and then follow the grassy footpath leading off slightly L. Bear further L to maintain a constant height walking through a small wood of Scots pine. The route continues SE, climbing slightly to reach the B6521 road. This is accessed via a swing gate. Cross the road on a diagonal to your R and then bear L through a gateway to re-enter the National Trust Longshaw Estate at a lodge. From here, continue SSW along the surfaced lane to arrive at the extensive Visitor and Information Centre, which contains a restaurant, shop and toilet facilities. Just before and below this centre there is a footpath with the sign 'No public access to Longshaw Meadow'. Take this path and a short distance down it pass through two swing gates in quick succession. At the second gate keep to the path directly ahead, avoiding a path off to the R which leads down to a pond. Further progress is then to the SSW along a wide gravel track.

The continuation way leads between two massive, pointed stone pillars and past a fenced-off area of deciduous woodland above to your L. Keep straight on when you come to an intersection of paths at a point where the boundary of the forested area climbs away. Your direction here continues SSW through a pleasant enclosed landscape. Beyond a gateway the views to your R become progressively more open and you can see Edale again, flanked by the silhouettes of Lose and Win Hills, on this occasion to the WNW. Keep to the main path and walk at a fairly constant elevation to reach the B6054 road at MR 260781 after passing through another swing gate. At this point, White Edge Moor (National Trust) looms ahead. Bear R along the nearside of the road to reach the Grouse Inn, a short distance further on.

The way to Baslow *(Allow 2½ hours)*

Turn R over the wooden stile just past the inn and then walk on a downhill diagonal to your L across the adjacent field to pass between a convenient gap in the stone walling ahead. Further progress is achieved across a more dilapidated stone wall and then down to another swing gate which breaches a more substantial wall. Turn immediately R

2:5 *Looking north-west towards Hathersage*

following this, pass over a P-stile and continue downhill adjacent to an extensive car parking area at Hay Wood (MR 256778), avoiding a side path leading down much more steeply on the R. Your own descent steepens to cross a small stream flowing across a bed of boulders and the way then rises again to connect with the B6054 road for a second time. This is reached up steps and accessed via a swing gate. Turn R and walk along the pavement before crossing the road on a diagonal to your L, at a point away from the bends and where you have maximum visibility of approaching traffic from both directions.

Use the gate to your L to take the sandy footpath that leads gently uphill through the Eastern Moors Estate to reach the northernmost point of Froggatt Edge, less than 1 km (about ½ mile) further on. During the easy climb to this edge, there are some superb views over to your R, from a massive boulder, looking back northwards towards Hathersage. Rose-bay willow-herb frames the foreground here. The way then leads through an uncomfortably tight K-gate to reach more open, flatter terrain. This marks the start of the rock face of Froggatt Edge, over which the buildings of Grindleford may be observed in the valley below, with the River Derwent meandering past them. This rocky edge of fantastically shaped buttresses and boulders merges with Curbar Edge to the south to provide an unbroken climbers' paradise extending for over 3 km (nearly 2 miles). Your continuation route is right beside it.

As you walk along Froggatt and Curbar Edges you will discover that there are plenty of side paths which loop right to the very edge of the rocky cliffs, providing safe vantage points for peering down into the depths below and observing expert climbers negotiating difficult overhangs. Watch where you place each of your own feet when approaching these exposed edges!

Further on, the tiny village of Froggatt is passed down below and there are many compelling viewpoints to inspect along the edge. Of all the times to be walking along this way, two of the best are in the autumn, when the heather is in bloom, and during freezing conditions when the then faded flowers attract a most delicate lace of frost.

All too soon the next minor road, that connecting the village of Curbar with the main A621 road, is reached. This is at MR 261747 near another large car park. Fortunately, more fine scenery lies ahead in the form of Baslow Edge and the path towards this is reached after crossing the road beyond a gaggle of gateways on your L. Through one of these, bear L along the main path avoiding a side path to the R which leads nearer to the edge. Sticking to the main path enables you

2:6 *Highland cattle around the Eagle Stone (Wellington's Monument in background)*

to inspect the Eagle Stone, a large, erratic boulder that is far more difficult to scale than it looks from the bottom, due to its protruding bevelled edges.

Your next destination is Wellington's Monument. This lies but a short distance to the SE and there is a direct path through the heathers. The monument is a fine affair and there are views across the wooded valley towards Gardom's Edge stretching away further southwards to link with the continuation edges above Chatsworth Park. Using the direction of your approach as a reference point, turn R at the monument and walk W along the wide-edged path. The continuation way then descends along a rough surface during which you must avoid a branch path off to the R by veering L to reach lower ground. Past a gate, proceed further downhill by means of a metalled road and continue past Hydro Close and Gorse Bank Lane along this road, now called School Lane, on reaching the outskirts of Baslow. After passing these, bear L down Eaton Hill to reach the centre of the conurbation at the village green in front of the Devonshire Arms. The village is well geared to the simple needs of walkers.

Alternatives

EXTENSIONS
The obvious extensions are to walk along more Edges to the N and S of the prescribed route.

To the N lies Stanage Edge and there is a variety of ways on to this escarpment at various points. Plan a route of your choice from Hathersage after consulting Pathfinder Map 743 (Sheffield). From the southernmost point of Stanage Edge make a point of visiting the Cowper Stone before connecting with the main route at Upper Burbage Bridge.

To the S lie Gardom's Edge, Dobb Edge and the high ground to the E of Chatsworth Park. Just continue southwards along these extended edges until you have had enough, before selecting a convenient way down into the lush parkland before back-tracking north-westwards into the village of Baslow.

EASIER ROUTES
The obvious short-cut is to miss out the northernmost section of the loop from Higger Tor. Walk S from the tor by way of the promontory of Carl Wark to connect again with the main route at the crossing of the A625 road at MR 263806.

Other escapes are possible towards the end of the route but these save only marginal distances, are relatively complicated to follow and are only sensible to use as a means of getting off the Edges early when faced with extremely adverse weather conditions.

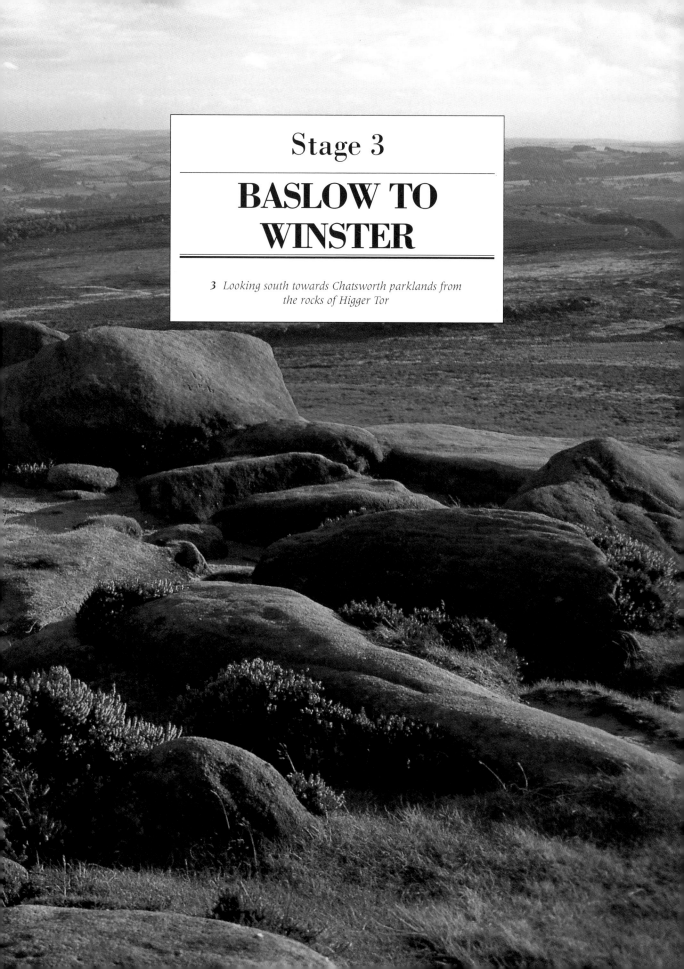

Stage 3

BASLOW TO WINSTER

*3 Looking south towards Chatsworth parklands from
the rocks of Higger Tor*

Stage 3: BASLOW to WINSTER

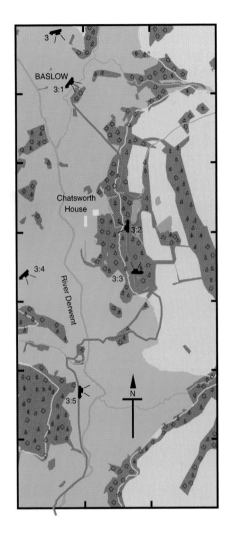

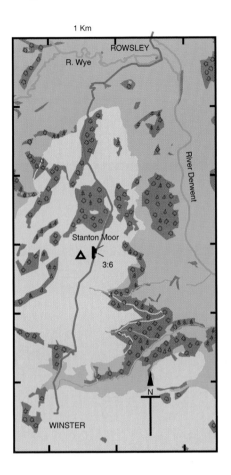

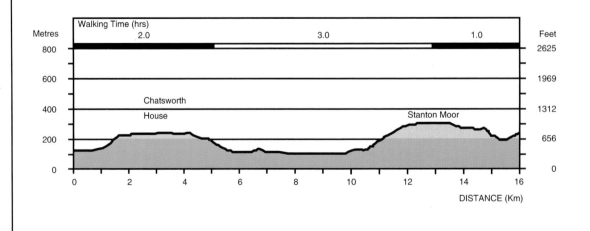

STARTING LOCATION

The village of Baslow at the junction of the
  A619, A623 and A621 roads to the N of
  Chatsworth Park.

OLM 24/MR258722.

Large car park with toilets.

Directions start from the car park at the centre
  of the village.

PUBLIC TRANSPORT

Hub of an extensive network of local and main
  line bus routes. There are connections with
  Ashford, Bakewell, Bradwell, Buxton,
  Castleton, Chapel-en-le-Frith, Chesterfield,
  Darley Dale, Doncaster, Eyam, Grindleford,
  Hartington, Hathersage, Hope, Litton,
  Macclesfield, Manchester, Matlock, New
  Mills, Rowsley, Sheffield, Stockport,
  Taddington, Wadshelf, Winster and
  Youlgreave; and other places!

OVERVIEW/INTEREST

A walk of great variety and never-ending
  interest.

An opportunity to explore Chatsworth House
  and parklands.

Good views throughout of both enclosed
  scenery and open landscpaes.

Delightful deciduous woodlands rich in flora
  and wildlife.

Section beside the River Derwent.

Route crosses the high ground of Stanton
  Moor with Nine Ladies Stone Circle.

FOOTPATHS/WAYSIGNS

The first part of the route is popular and
  adequately signposted over firm ground and
  mainly follows well-established footpaths.

This progressively deteriorates towards the end
  of the stage and the final approach to
  Winster is challenging in that it is much less
  frequently used, there are few signs and in
  wet weather several areas of boggy, waterlogged ground have to be crossed, one of
  which (a small, muddy watercourse) will
  severely test your 'hopping across' skills!

There is a virtual absence of erosion.

OVERALL TIME ALLOWANCE 6 hours

Statistics		
Distance walked	**Km**	**Miles**
	16.0	9.9
Height climbed	**M**	**Feet**
	420	1375
Principal heights	**M**	**Feet**
Edge above Chatsworth	240	785
Stanton Moor (trig point)	323	1060

The way to Beeley Hilltop (MR 268685)
(Allow 2 hours)

Turn R out of the car park and cross the stream, Bar Brook, by the
stone hump-backed bridge. Turn immediately R along the public footpath signed to 'Chatsworth' and walk S, passing by an attractive
terrace of thatched cottages. Avoid passing through a K-gate leading
off on your R and follow the main path which will bring you to an
imposing wrought-iron gateway, one of the entrances to the parklands surrounding Chatsworth House. There are several diagonal
ways across these exquisite, sheltered parklands with their assortment
of specimen trees but the one suggested is the concession path signed

to 'Stand Tower 1 ml and Beeley 3½ mls'. This leads SE towards the edge above Chatsworth House. To start with, there is a faint cart-track to follow, but this soon peters out in the lush turf and you will then have to select your own diagonal. This delightful section of the way leads round and beneath a scattering of mature deciduous trees including horse chestnuts, oak, sycamore, ash and cherries.

Further on, the main surfaced approach drive to the House is crossed and after this there are more open views, the most spectacular of which is the one of distant Birchen/Gardom's Edge ahead on your L to the NNE. Ahead on the R, the tip of Stand Tower (a former hunting lodge which you will visit later) appears to the SSW, towering above the densely wooded slopes. Head for a gap between two clumps of trees to cross a wide gravel track. Past this, bear L towards the rising ground on your L, still maintaining your SE bearing. The way continues under further mature trees, just clipping a group of beech and sycamore. The approach diagonal then leads towards a pronounced grassy bank beyond which there is a stone boundary wall with an S-stile positioned in it. Trim your final approach to converge on this stile. One landmark to look for near this important exit is a low wooden form and a protective sapling oak tree; these are at MR 265712. Climb over the stile and continue up the clear path of compacted earth which leads up the wooded slope ahead, initially extending your SE approach diagonal.

3:1 Departing from Baslow across Blake Brook

3:2 *Above the water cascades at Chatsworth House*

The way then bears more to the s beneath a cooling canopy of foliage which supports a variety of bird and animal life. This part of the route is particularly attractive in May when the ground is blanketed by bluebells. Your upwards diagonal leads to a forest road running N to S along the edge of the escarpment. Bear R along this superior way, walking s in the direction signed 'Concession Footpath – Stand Tower – Beeley 2½ Mls'. The way then leads to Stand Tower, where you need to bear R in order to inspect the building and its observation turrets. From the edge just beyond the tower there are really impressive views of Chatsworth House down below and the tiny village of Edensor across the Parklands. However, the well-maintained former hunting lodge is now a private residence and should be respected as such.

Retrace your final approach steps back to the main N-to-S forest track, before turning R along it to resume progress towards 'Hob Hurst's House and Beeley', as signed. This is to the SSE. Bear L at the next fork to follow the direction indicated by a purple arrow daubed on a large stone. From here, the way leads round the northern tip of Emperor Lake set within dense woodlands. Just past this indent, be particularly careful to locate and turn along a narrow path to your R which winds southwards round the eastern fringe of the lake. The lake attracts many species of birds, including waterfowl, and your passage through thick undergrowth allows camouflaged observations

at relatively close quarters. All too soon you will reach the southern tip of the lake but to do this be careful always to keep to the narrow path nearest to the edge of the water; ignore all side paths leading away to your L. Bear R round the tip of the lake, again spurning all ways off to the L. The route then leads towards a small jetty at which a dinghy is often moored but, before reaching this, turn L along the obvious continuation track as the path round the lake comes to an abrupt end. Turn L again at the T-junction ahead to resume your direction of travel southwards along the forest way. (For those walkers in a hurry, the loop round Emperor Lake may be ignored by simply keeping to the main forest track leading southwards.)

Just ahead there is a memorable view through the trees on your R, where a stubby branch path will take you to an observation point adjacent to the tiny holding pool feeding the water cascades that fall dramatically through the landscaped gardens of Chatsworth House. You will find this view at MR 266701. There are some potentially dangerous fall-aways at this spot, so always keep a tight hand-grip on any youngsters in your group.

3:3 Walking through the deciduous woodlands above Chatsworth Park

Resume your progress s along the edge through shady woodland. Initially this is through a long, fairly straight section. The route then tracks slightly downhill to reach a major service road through the estate. Veer L at this junction in the opposite direction to that indicated on another purple arrow marker. A short distance further on, bear R along a wide, grassy path to resume walking s. You will then join another gravel-surfaced service track along which you turn R. This leads to a gate and P-stile at the boundary wall of the estate.

Over the stile, the scenery changes dramatically and the vastness of the higher ground of Beeley Moor stretches away up the slopes to your L. However, after walking no more than about 100 paces in this direction, bear off R, downhill, following a narrow waymarked path (this is signed 'Beeley + Calton Lees'). A pleasant traverse descends across bracken-covered slopes to reach sheltered pastures below. The way leads to an elaborate configuration of stiles at a wooden gate, the new superseding the remains of the previous crossing of the high stone walling. Beyond this obstacle, cross the adjacent field on a downwards continuation diagonal to your L, heading WSW towards the farm buildings below. Another S-stile provides entry to a farm lane down which you turn R. The buildings ahead signify that you have reached Beeley Hilltop and the lane leads round them in a loop to their R. There are groups of unusual toadstool-shaped stone pillars hereabouts. These are 'staddle stones' and were formally used to support grain stores and raise them from the ground; the shape of these supports was designed to keep out vermin.

3:4 *A crisp winter's morning in frosty Chatsworth Park*

The way to Stanton Moor (Nine Ladies Stone Circle) *(Allow 3 hours)*

A steep descent along the minor lane leads to Beeley Lodge. Beyond the lodge, turn R along the B6012 road to cross over the River Derwent at the arched stone pack-horse bridge where the heavy flow of modern traffic is controlled by lights. A more imposing entrance to Chatsworth Park lies just ahead; near this, veer L and cross a wide gravel path exclusively reserved for anglers. Continue up the slope directly ahead, walking SW round a wooded area. The path splits along here, but either branch will bring you to a macadam road by which there are extensive car parking areas. Cross this road and then bear L along the lane ahead, walking in the direction signed 'Chatsworth Forest Office and Sawmill 200 yards on left'. These are soon passed to your L near a point where the lane bends sharply R. Motorists are advised to 'Hoot' here.

The lane will bring you to a junction of ways at a small grass triangle. Bear L at this division to walk southwards, uphill, passing in quick succession Calton Lees Farm, Moor View and Calton Lees House. These signify that you are about to depart from the tiny settlement of Calton Lees at MR 257681. Immediately after passing these dwellings, bear slightly L and use the S-stile to gain access to the footpath signed to 'Rowsley'. Along the brow ahead there are fine, open views of the wooded River Derwent valley; far away, the heights above Beeley dominate the skyline. A grassy path takes you further southwards as the hamlet of Beeley comes into view over the stone wall on your L. You need to cross this wall a short distance further on at a wooden L-stile. From here, the way descends gently SSW across lush cattle meadows.

The obvious way then passes through a gateway and across more meadows where a side path off to the L must be avoided. After passing through a gateway in a stone wall, the broad, grassy way veers L and then tracks beside the tree-lined River Derwent for a short stretch. The way then veers away from the river to lead you to a wooden P-stile at another stone wall, this one to your R. The narrowing path then winds through an enclosed strip of shrubbery where it is quite often muddy. Fortunately, a stile to the L of a gate provides a rapid escape from this wet ground. More open fields lie ahead, and a short distance further on some buildings come into sight above to your L, signifying that you are approaching Rowsley. However, there is more heavy going to contend with before you reach this village. The worst of this is beneath trees, alongside the river, where there are often several areas that are extremely boggy and difficult to avoid. Do not be tempted to make more than the most cursory deviation uphill to your R in seeking the most agreeable route through the morass along the wide path, as most of the deep mud will soon be left behind.

The route then continues further sw along a drier grassy way and this becomes upgraded to a track as the silhouette of the church of St Katherine is seen to your R. The track then passes beneath an arched railway bridge (which also spans the River Derwent at this point). Next, climb over the stone S-stile near the gate ahead and then turn L along the lane on the other side to pass Granby Cottage. The lane leads to the main A6(T) road, which needs to be crossed with care opposite the Peacock Hotel. On the far side of the A6(T), continue along the road signed 'Stanton in the Peak 1½' and 'Caudwell's Mill and Craft Centre'. Continue past the nearby car park and the signed attractions and cross the River Wye before bearing full R with the road in the direction signed to 'Pilhough ¾ Stanton in the Peak 1½'. A play area is then passed to your L. At the next L-hand bend in the road, select the public footpath by keeping straight ahead and climbing over a stile to the R of a gate. The footpath bears L uphill along a grassy track away from the valley floor and the river. Your direction up this shallow gradient is wsw, veering further s higher up.

Continue upwards along the track. As further height is gained there are attractive views back downhill towards Rowsley in its tranquil setting of gentle, wooded hills and pastures. The straight edge marking the higher ground of Beeley Moor rises on the distant horizon to the NE. Further on, change direction slightly by bearing R to follow the signed public way which is to the wsw across extensive meadows. Then head for the far L-hand corner of a boundary stone wall to locate and pass through a wooden stile set into the walling before reaching the corner. Following this, bear R downhill to cross in quick succession another stile, a small stream and a gate, with the help of some well-positioned concrete blocks. Then turn R before following the contours of the hill round to your L, arriving at Dove House Farm which is entered through a G-stile next to a gateway. The farm is reached at MR 247653.

At the farm, turn L up the twisting, narrow lane passing the farmhouse to your R. The lane contorts up the steep slope ahead and the buildings of Congreave are soon left behind. Near the top of the brow be extremely vigilant to locate a stile on your R which is sometimes boarded across. Use this stile to continue up the grassy slopes to the ssw and select an angle which will lead you directly to a G-stile in the corner of the field on your L. Beyond this, continue tracking ssw up the shallow slopes of a gully towards the woodlands above, now in sight on your L. The ground ahead then rises more steeply. Pass through a convenient gap in an intervening stone wall to reach another minor lane above, accessed by means of a stile to your L. Turn R along the lane. Just beyond Beighton Lodge turn L off the lane up a narrow footpath which skirts the woodlands (Sheepwalk Wood) that cover the rising slope ahead. This turning is at MR 246648. The path initially leads SSE and then tracks to SSW, keeping towards the fringe of the

Left: 3:5 *A tranquil scene near Rowsley*

trees. The exact line of the path becomes obscure in places; where this occurs, use the edge of the woodlands as a guide.

A steady climb follows, under a leafy canopy that is particularly welcome on a hot, sunny day. (However, the best time to walk up these slopes is on a crisp day in autumn just after the leaves have started to fall.) Towards the top of the rise, veer further R along a wider path that leads you to a narrow lane. Turn L down the lane and walk E for about 100 paces. Then turn off to follow the public footpath to your R signed to 'Stone Circle'. A well-used track then leads S and a distinct landmark is a communications pylon on the skyline ahead to your R. A wide sandy path then threads through bracken, gorse and heather shaded by silver birch, oak and beech trees. There are several gates with S-stiles or G-stiles to be negotiated before eventually reaching the stone circle in a clearing off to your R at MR 249635. It is marked on the OLM as 'Nine Ladies Stone Circle'.

Below: 3:6 *Looking east towards Matlock from the heights of Stanton Moor*

The way to Winster *(Allow 1 hour)*

Continue s from the stone circle to penetrate the higher, more exposed ground of Stanton Moor. In clear weather, there are good views down into Darley Dale and of the sprawling town of Matlock, far away on your L beyond the heather-clad slopes of the moor. Unusually, these open slopes support isolated clumps of rhododendrons in addition to heather and bracken. The wide, sandy path is a joy to skip along and fast progress is possible across and down from the moor.

From the main path, there are diagonal side paths off to the R which will lead you to the trig point a short distance above. This commands a height of 323 m (1060 ft) and is only a minor deviation from your route s, as too is the short additional loop to visit and perhaps climb up the massive boulder, the 'Cork Stone', at MR 243628. (Steps and iron hand grips are provided.)

After these minor diversions, leave the moor along the main path which, having crossed another one running at right angles, leads SSW over falling terrain to a minor road at MR 246625. The road is accessed via a wooden stile. Veer R along this lane and within 50 paces select the continuation footpath leading off to the L. This leads through a more sheltered landscape down to and round Barn Farm. The farmyard is entered through a G-stile to the L of a wide metal gate. Through this, walk round and below the farm to pass through a second such G-stile towards the far end of the buildings. Proceed further s along the signed footpath, ignoring another path off to your R. Enticing meadows stretch ahead: make a point here of keeping to the R-hand edge of the first of these and squeeze through an important narrow G-stile in the wall at the far end. Continue downhill from here, veering R in doing so. Then ignore another side path on your R leading away through a G-stile. Cross a waterlogged area and the often muddy approach track to Uppertown Farm. At this point you will find a new sign informing you that ahead lies Winster whilst to your rear is Birchover.

Leave the boggy track through the R of two gateways and walk slightly uphill along a tractor-rutted path. The direction is still to the s. When the tractor tracks veer away to the R, continue straight ahead, keeping near the hawthorn hedge on your L. Ignore a track further on which aborts L through an iron gate. Beyond the obscure G-stile ahead, the path bends sharply R and from here a fairly straight diagonal leads downhill across the slope along a narrow way. At the end of this section, bear L to continue more directly downhill passing through another narrow gap in a stone wall ahead. During this descent there are fine views of the valley below and of the outline of some of the buildings of Winster sprawling along the top of the far hillside. The route continues across some exacting, waterlogged ground and fords a small brook with deep, muddy banks. After heavy rain be prepared to get your feet wet for here the main objective is not to slip right in.

You will soon reach drier slopes. The way then continues more steeply downhill and crosses the valley bottom. An obvious way then leads back uphill passing through several more stiles and across further boggy ground (although not quite so severe as that encountered on the way down) into the charming village of Winster. Before reaching the village, your path connects with a surfaced track which leads to Woodhouse Lane. Continue straight ahead up this narrow lane past a row of cottages to reach the village's main street, a wide boulevard. You will find much of interest in Winster.

Alternatives

EXTENSIONS

Beyond the southern end of Chatsworth Park, the main route is fairly direct across the only intervening high ground between this point and Winster to the s. Therefore, opportunities for either extensions or short-cuts during the latter part of the stage are somewhat limited. You are advised to plan your variations (if any) within the confines and immediate surroundings of Chatsworth Park.

One obvious extension is from near the southern entrance to the Park, at MR 260684. Turn R along the footpath leading northwards beside the River Derwent to reach and visit Chatsworth House. Then proceed to the village of Edensor to inspect the spired church of St Peter's. The churchyard has important connections with the United States of America; see if you can discover what these are! The tiny, immaculately kept village also boasts a shop/post-office/café/ – a welcome oasis for hungry or thirsty walkers. There is a good path from Edensor which leads first uphill on a ssw diagonal, then on the flat through a narrow strip of woodlands (New Piece Wood), round Calton Houses and finally downhill to reconnect with the main route at Calton Lees.

Another possibility is at Beeley Hilltop. Instead of descending straight to Beeley Lodge, loop southwards to visit the delightful village of Beeley before returning to the main route at the crossing of the River Derwent by back-tracking NNW along the footpath which converges on the east bank of the river.

EASIER ROUTES

The best short-cut is to miss out the climb to the higher ground to the E above Chatsworth Park. Simply walk s through the lower parkland, visiting the House and ornamental gardens en route. Keep heading s along the paths which follow the course of the river, to reconnect with the main route at MR 260684.

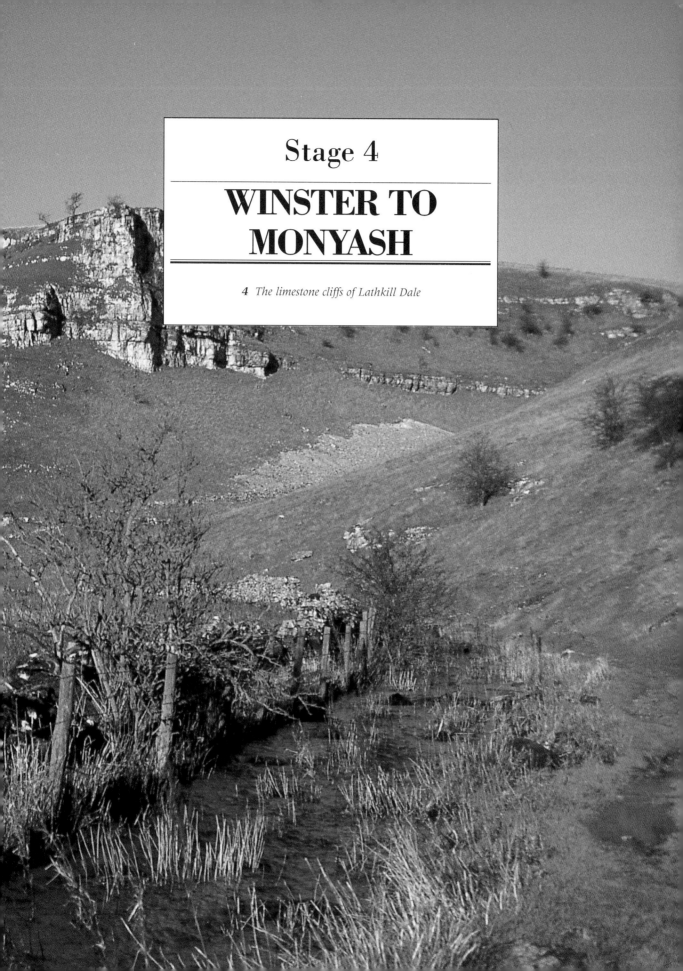

Stage 4

WINSTER TO MONYASH

4 *The limestone cliffs of Lathkill Dale*

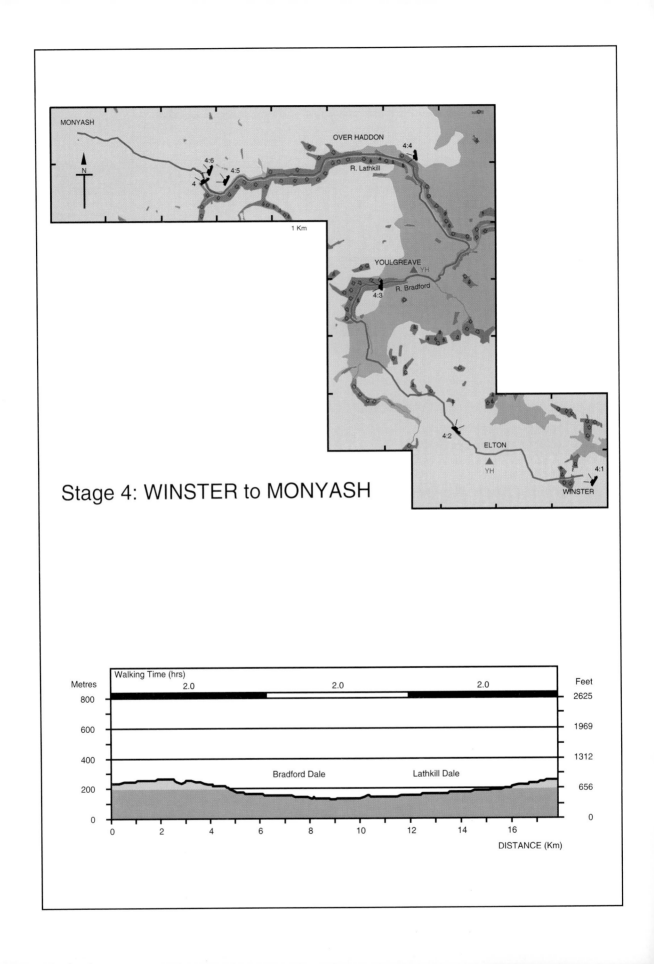

MONYASH

N

OVER HADDON

4:4

R. Lathkill

4:6

4:5

4

1 Km

YOULGREAVE ▲ YH

R. Bradford

4:3

4:2

ELTON

▲ YH

4:1

WINSTER

Stage 4: WINSTER to MONYASH

Walking Time (hrs)			
	2.0	2.0	2.0

Metres									Feet
800									2625
600									1969
400				Bradford Dale		Lathkill Dale			1312
200									656
0									0

0   2   4   6   8   10   12   14   16

DISTANCE (Km)

STARTING LOCATION

Winster on the B5057 road between Bakewell and Matlock.

OLM 24/MR 242605

No dedicated car park in village centre but parking tolerated along the sides of the wide main street. Alternative parking at top of West Bank.

Directions start from the main street, outside the National Trust's Market House.

PUBLIC TRANSPORT

Bus routes 57B, 170 (Chesterfield, Baslow, Bakewell) and 172 (Bakewell, Stanton, Winster, Matlock).

OVERVIEW/INTEREST

Pleasant, undulating rural landscapes at start.

The highlight must be walking along Bradford and Lathkill Dales.

Breathtaking limestone scenery including cliffs, tors, towers, screes, sunken watercourses, caves and rock-falls.

Abundant wildlife beside the tranquil flows of the rivers Bradford and Lathkill – in, on and above the water.

The exposed sandstone faces of the disused quarry on Anthony Hill will appeal to those interested in geology.

Attractive villages of Winster, Elton, Youlgreave, Bradford, Alport, Over Haddon and Monyash.

FOOTPATHS/WAYSIGNS

Somewhat of a mixture.

Along the dales, good to excellent, on refurbished paths that are reasonably well signed.

Route finding to Bradford Dale is relatively complicated, with few helpful waysigns where these are most needed.

Virtually no erosion anywhere; one rock-fall coming out of Lathkill Dale which is easily negotiated along a path across the jumble of boulders.

Some wet and boggy areas but no real problems.

OVERALL TIME ALLOWANCE 6 hours

Statistics		
Distance walked	**Km**	**Miles**
	17.8	11.1
Height climbed	**M**	**Feet**
	200	655
Principal heights	**M**	**Feet**
Anthony Hill	293	960
(Summit not visited)		
Monyash	270	885

The way to Bradford Dale *(Allow 2 hours)*

From Winster Market Hall (National Trust property) walk W along Main Street, passing the post-office. Turn L up West Bank thus avoiding the continuation road signed to 'Bakewell Ashbourne (B5056)' and 'Elton Newhaven'. Then turn immediately R down the public footpath, passing a notice board dedicated to St John the Baptist Church, Winster. Pass through the graveyard above the church and, ahead, select the higher of a choice of paths. The church is in a beautiful, peaceful setting and the best views of it are from a short distance further on, looking back from a secluded dell. To reach this spot, leave the churchyard through a narrow G-stile to continue WSW across the wooded glade with the outline of the church peeping through the

4:1 *Early morning sunshine on a frosty Winster*

foliage behind you. The way continues up the brow of the hillock ahead beside a wire fence to your R. Cross the next meadow where there are more views of the undulating, wooded countryside. Through two more G-stiles and beyond the next meadow the B5056 road is reached by means of an S-stile over a stone wall. This connection is at MR 235605.

Cross the road on a diagonal to your R to reach the continuation footpath on the other side, accessed by stone steps and a wooden stile. The way continues westwards across meadowland and passes through another G-stile; then it follows the course of a dry-stone wall and passes a dilapidated barn to your R. The dominating higher ground away to the NNE (to your R rear), is the upthrust of Stanton Moor, rising above the elongated village of Birchover. The next part of the way is often quite muddy in wet weather but these patches are soon left behind as the obvious way tracks slightly uphill, passing through a stone wall at a G-stile, after which it veers marginally to the R and to the WNW. It then connects with the Limestone Way at MR 232605, through another G-stile. The Way is well signed: turn R along it to continue NW. Along the wide, walled track, the distinctive buildings on the hillside to your L are those of Westhill Farm. Further on, pass another derelict barn to your R. Beyond this the harshness of the retaining walls is camouflaged by shrubbery containing hawthorn, hazel, beech and brambles.

When you reach the minor road ahead, it is necessary to leave the Limestone Way by turning L and following the road into the narrow village of Elton, less than 0.5km (about ¼mile) away to the W. Proceed along the main street of the little village, passing the YHA hostel on your L and the fine building of All Saints Church to your R. Turn R down Well Street, next to the churchyard, and then select the public footpath signed to 'Youlgreave' by bearing L a short distance further on. (This footpath is initially a wide car track between dwellings.) When this track bends sharply to the R, leave it by passing through a gap on your L next to a metal gate. This turning is indicated by a yellow waymarker. Keep well over to the L and ease your way gingerly along by the stone wall to avoid the worst of what is a quagmire in all but the driest of seasons. Sooner or later you are forced to find a way across as you need to strike off R to walk down the often slippery grassy slopes further on, following the L one of two paths to reach the narrow lane down below at MR 218613. As you tread carefully down the slopes there are open views ahead of your approach towards the escarpment of Anthony Hill, which you will soon be walking round. On the way to the lane, glance to your R at the rocky outcrop named Robin Hood's Stride, the tip of which is just visible to the NNE. (This is quite close and a visit to it is suggested in the Extensions section on pages 82-83.) There are further stiles and usually more mud to contend with before the lane is reached.

Bear R along the lane, walking NNW directly towards Anthony Hill. Ignore the next footpath on your L and continue up rising ground towards the escarpment. When the lane bends to the R, leave it by following the public footpath on your L, signed to 'Youlgreave 2½'. This is accessed through a G-stile to the R of a barred gate. Follow the narrow path as it winds up the scarp slope. Ahead, a short looped detour off to the R will bring you face to face with some fascinating sandstone beds exposed by abandoned quarrying operations. (Watch and listen

4:2 *Exposed sandstone bedding planes at disused quarry, Anthony Hill*

out for motor bikes as this general area of blind hillocks is used by scramblers.) On reaching the far end of the interesting bits of the quarry, return to the main path down to the L and then, from a choice of ways, be very careful to continue along the lower path that leads NW. (Do use your compass here to check your continuation direction!) The correct way leads to a complicated double wooden G- and S-stile near the corner of a stone wall.

You escape from the quarry is completed along a grassy way that leads slightly uphill beside a dilapidated stone wall and then L downhill, through clumps of gorse bushes, towards Rock Farm, through which the route passes. This is at MR 211619 just below a dense coppice. During your descent you will see the deep, wooded V-nick of Gratton Dale winding away to the SW.

As you approach the farm, always keep to the higher ground in order to avoid the worst of several muddy areas on your semi-circular way down along a faintly defined narrow path. Be vigilant here not to deviate S and below the official route of the footpath. Quite often there are horses grazing in this vicinity. A rectangular stone pillar, to the L of a gap in a stone wall, marks the way; beyond this, a P-stile signals the entrance to more enclosed, scrubby ground, through which there is a better defined path. Then after crossing a stile straddling a barbed wire fence and having passed through a metal gate, you pass above the buildings of Rock Farm.

Continue W along the farm track to reach a minor lane ahead at a hairpin bend. Bear L down this lane but after about 120 paces be particularly vigilant to detect and turn off along a narrow, partly concealed footpath on your R (which in autumn 1994 was not sign-posted). Your new direction is to the NW, more directly towards Bradford Dale, which is your next major objective some 1.5 km (1 mile) away. The next section is overgrown and can be quite muddy but press on to reach more open ground beyond another G-stile. More waterlogged rough ground has to be crossed before another wooden stile is reached that straddles a wire fence, the top strand of which is barbed so take care crossing it!

From here, continue NNW along a clearer, grassy way that passes beneath overhead cables as the going improves. Cross beneath these cables before reaching the next gate, veering W to follow the contours of the slope downhill to your L, below Beech Wood. Then be particularly careful to locate and pass through a wooden stile to the L of a metal gate at the bottom of the shallow valley near to the small water-course. Cross this stream by the narrow stone bridge at MR 202626, where the word 'Tumulus' is positioned on the OLM but not on the ground. Turn R along the farm track on the other side to cross a more powerful watercourse and after about 40 paces be vigilant to turn off to the R over another wooden stile, this one leading awkwardly away from your direction of approach.

(Route finding along this last described section of the stage is quite exacting and a plea to the local authority is that some helpful signs and other improvements to the pathways are initiated as soon as possible. There has already been a positive response to this plea in that the landowners have agreed that the line of the path should be way-marked and this will be done.)

Continue due N along a relatively easy-to-follow grassy path down the wide valley, leaving a barn behind on your R. The better defined way leads across meadows directly towards a clump of conifer trees that marks your intended connection with the southerly reaches of Bradford Dale. Numerous stone walls bar your way and these are crossed by conveniently positioned S-stiles. The way leads directly to a stone bridge spanning a wider stream in a shallow, tree-covered gully. Across the water, turn sharp L to walk W along the deepening cleft, now below on your L. When you reach the 'No right of way' sign ahead, tread carefully down the steep flight of steps at which a protective handrail has been positioned. Bear R at the bottom to follow the obvious wide path that winds westwards along the valley. Cross the stream again by the narrow concrete bridge a short distance further on. As you continue down the wooded valley sandwiched between precipitous slopes, you are walking into Bradford Dale.

4:3 *The tranquillity of Bradford Dale*

The way to below Over Haddon *(Allow 2 hours)*

Turn R when you reach a T-junction ahead. This is away from the direction signed to 'Middleton'. About 2 km (1¼ miles) of sheer delight lie immediatley ahead as you track northwards along Bradford Dale. This is on really good paths and beneath the intermingled foliage of many varieties of deciduous tree. In this part of your journey you pass a succession of weirs, each one different but all supporting wildlife that includes fish, frogs, ducks and other birds, and several species of mammal. Continue down the dale ignoring a footpath off to your L over a walled bridge. There are some restrictive notices further along the dale but none of these should bother you unless you intend to fish without permission, or fancy bathing or have a dog with you but have forgotten to bring a lead!

Further down the widening dale you will see some buildings lining the top of the steep slopes on your L; these are part of Youlgreave, which you pass below but do not have to walk through. Swift progress is now possible, downstream, along the wide, renovated path and at MR 640209 the river Bradford is crossed by a stone footbridge spanning a shallow, pebbly stretch of the stream. Just up Holywell Lane from here is Meadow Cottage Tea Room, where you will be given a warm welcome by this well-patronized establishment with its inviting 'Teas and Hovis' sign from a bygone era. Through the narrow G-stile at the bottom of the lane, continue eastwards down the progressively widening dale to reach the outskirts of the village of Bradford at twin wooden gates. Pass through the G-stile here; ignore the adjacent footpath across the river to your R; cross the minor road at MR 640213, pass through the G-stile opposite and continue along the track which then bends to the L beside the course of a stream.

Pass rocky, limestone bluffs as you cross the stream again. Further on, walk past an arched stone bridge near which there is an all-weather bench beneath an overhanging limestone ledge. The dedication here reads: 'In loving memory of Harold Lee 1918–1989 The Man with the crooked stick.' Follow the way along the valley, making good use of all grassy detours to avoid continuously walking along the surfaced track. Your direction in doing this is NE. A short distance further on, after having passed through either a K-gate or a G-stile, your route approaches a pronounced limestone cliff partly concealed by trees. The way bends round this formidable crag and just past this feature you reach the minor road through Alport, having passed through another G-stile and recrossed the stream. Cross the road using the two G-stiles to gain entry and exit.

Continue along the path which is signed to 'Conksbury'. This is about a kilometre (½ mile) upstream. You are now treading along the

4:4 *The cascading weirs in lower Lathkill Dale*

SE tip of Lathkill Dale, which you will follow for about the next 7 km (4½ miles) as it wanders westwards, changing in character from a wide, shallow valley to a spectacular limestone gorge lined with steep cliffs, towers, watersinks, screes and rock-falls. The first section gives little hint of the splendours to come as you walk within a landscape of rounded slopes grazed by sheep. Numerous G-stiles come and go along the obvious path, waymarked with yellow arrowheads, and the most interesting views along this stretch are to your R across the River Lathkill as it winds beneath a steep, wooded escarpment. Beyond about the ninth G-stile the way begins to climb gently uphill through an area of sparse trees beside a limestone wall on your L. It signals the approach to the lane passing through Conksbury and this is reached higher up after having passed through two more stiles (one a gap and one a step). This connection is at MR 212655.

Turn R down the lane to cross the river at the narrow, walled Conksbury Bridge, keeping a wary eye on traffic which approaches from both directions. Safely over, turn immediately L to continue along signed route No. 3 further up Lathkill Dale, still progressing westwards. A short distance further on, the buildings of Over Haddon can be seen on the skyline directly ahead, but your intended route, if not obstructed passes well below these as it hugs the floor of the dale.

4:5 *The exposed limestone crags of upper Lathkill Dale*

Vegetation now increases along the banks of the river and also up the steep sides of the ever-deepening dale where trees cling tenaciously to the thin alkaline soil of the inhospitable slopes. Beyond an enormous K-gate, the dale sweeps graciously to the L past a series of weirs, the fall of the highest being less than a metre.

Rapid progress is again possible along the excellent path. While you are stepping out along here there is little time to admire the splendid scenery or to register the speed with which the skyline of Over Haddon is being passed, high above to your R. The very obvious way leads over a W-stile, through a gate and along an embankment to reach the end of a narrow lane that leads up to Over Haddon. This is at MR 203662, at Lathkill Lodge. Normally you would not have to make use of the lane here, but read on! Turn R away from the river at this point which is opposite a footbridge. Then bear almost immediately L to pass through a gate as a preliminary to making use of the concession part of the footpath up Lathkill Dale. However, there is a restrictive notice at the entry point which reads: 'This private footpath is closed for shooting on several occasions from October to January.' I have been there on two such occasions, when an additional notice reads: 'Danger no access beyond this point shooting in progress.'

The way to Monyash (Allow 2 hours)

If the permanent notice only is in place, proceed with confidence up the dale along the concession path. (If the second notice is also there, you will have no alternative but to make a detour by way of Over Haddon – see Extensions p.82.) The concession way leads for over 2 km (about 1¼ miles) through extensive woodlands, the westerly part of which is Palmerston Wood. Leave the restricted 'shooting area' at a stile and wooden gate that separate a stone wall and a wire fence. Continue westwards into spectacular limestone scenery, walking past more weirs over which volumes of water cascade after heavy rains. Beyond the second of these, the steep R-hand slopes of the dale are lined with limestone buttresses and tors which reveal their horizontal layering, deposited by tiny fossilized animals (crinoids) over millions of years. Beneath these impressive outcrops, loose scree slopes drop down sharply into the now deep dale. Beyond another W-stile the dale becomes wilder and more craggy still as the steep sides converge and you pass through a narrowing gorge.

After you have crossed a wooden P-stile, the volume of water in the river noticeably diminishes as several feeder streams are passed. Below a particularly sharp-edged limestone outcrop, a dry dale joins from the R opposite another leading in from the L as the main valley sweeps L further upstream beyond. The rocky side dale to the R leads up to Haddon Grove; the other leading S is the narrow, wooded indent

of Calling Low Dale. Keep to the R-hand side of the river ignoring all side paths off to the R and bridges across the stream to the L. Having passed the entrance to Cales Dale where a footbridge over the river should be ignored, the route leads to a cave below a cliff to your L where the stream first emerges into the open. Continue westwards up the now dry dale along a rough, stony path and up a gradient which steepens marginally. The path then swings across the floor of the rising valley to continue along the L-hand side of the now narrow and enclosed dale. Limestone cliffs, rocks, boulders and scree intermingle along the next section as the distinct narrow path threads a clear way along the bottom of the dale. At one point this passes to the L, round and over a significant rock-fall.

The characteristics of the dale change abruptly again as the rock features give way to gentle grassy slopes. The still rising dale declines in depth. Past occasional W-stiles the clearly defined path leads to the B5055 road, E of the village of Monyash. Turn L along this and complete the stage by walking the short distance along the road into the attractive village, which is entered along Church Street. The enterprising proprietor of the Old Smithy Tea Rooms and Café (next to the Bull's Head) has a real empathy with the needs of walkers: breakfast is served all day, you can obtain a daily paper there and 'Muddy boots are welcome!'

4:6 *Morning sunshine highlights the waters of the River Lathkill*

Alternatives

EXTENSIONS
First, the compulsory detour when 'shooting' is in progress in Lathkill Dale: turn back at the entrance to the concession way near Lathkill

Lodge and walk up the lane leading steeply into Over Haddon. Pass the car park and toilets by veering L; turn L at the T-junction ahead and walk westwards along the minor road. About 1.5 km (1 mile) further on, at MR 191664, bear L along the back lane signed to 'Haddon Grove 1'. Pass Mandale House (which offers accommodation). Further on when the lane bends acutely to the R, bear off L towards Haddon Grove Farm by going through a wide gateway. Walk SW between the extensive farm buildings in the direction waysigned. There is now a choice of ways and the one recommended continues to head SW back towards Lathkill Dale to reconnect with the main route at the bottom of the dale at MR 174655. There are two reasons for this choice. Firstly the views westwards along Lathkill Dale from the top are magnificent. Although you are faced with a steep climb down, there is a very adequate path which contains stepped sections – and when you reach the bottom you can walk up the remaining part of the dale to the W with its many arresting limestone features. The second reason is that the alternative higher level path across country (which you access by turning sharp R at the end of the farm buildings and then continuing on a NW diagonal) crosses numerous high stone walls by means of a most frustrating combination of awkward, slippery step stiles.

One extension is to visit the jumble of boulders named Robin Hood's Stride at MR 224622. This is only a short detour from the section of the main route between the village of Elton and Anthony Hill and can be completed as a relatively quick 'there and back', leaving the main route at MR 221611 and returning to it at MR 217614, using a combination of footpaths and a convenient minor road.

A longer extension is to visit Haddon Hall and Park. This can be conveniently achieved from the vicinity of Alport and you can loop back to the main route through Lathkill Dale via Over Haddon. You can select one of several alternative ways of including this detour by consulting the OLM.

EASIER ROUTES

A less interesting (in that it misses out most of the scenery of Bradford and Lathkill Dales) and less strenuous route is to follow the Limestone Way for longer in its progress towards Monyash. The described main route departs from this Way at MR 229611 by turning off W towards the village of Elton. However, you could continue northwards along the Way as far as Bradford Dale and then either follow the main route through Lathkill Dale or continue along the Limestone Way right into Monyash. It is recommended that you choose the first of these two alternatives when you reach Bradford Dale because the walk through Lathkill Dale should not be missed and the section of the Limestone Way from Bradford Dale to Monyash, although waysigned, is quite complicated to follow.

Stage 5

MONYASH TO ILAM/THORPE

5 Above Dove Dale

Stage 5: MONYASH to ILAM/THORPE

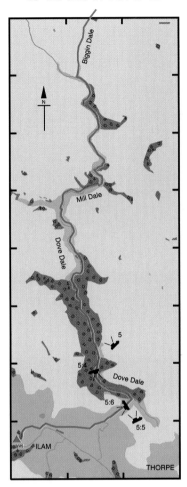

MONYASH

5:1

5:2

5:3

Biggin Dale

N

1 Km

Biggin Dale

Mill Dale

Dove Dale

5

5:4

Dove Dale

5:6

5:5

ILAM

THORPE

N

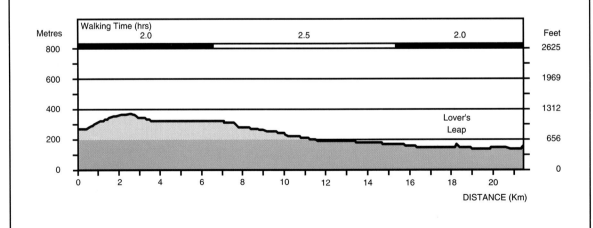

Metres	Walking Time (hrs)			Feet
	2.0	2.5	2.0	
800				2625
600				1969
400			Lover's Leap	1312
200				656
0				0

DISTANCE (Km)

0   2   4   6   8   10   12   14   16   18   20

STARTING LOCATION

The village of Monyash situated just off the A515, on the B5055 road to Bakewell.

OLM 24/MR 150666.

Small car park near centre of village holds about 15 cars.

Directions start from village green.

PUBLIC TRANSPORT

Bus routes 57 (Macclesfield, Buxton, Ashbourne/Matlock), 177 (Bakewell/Friden, Flagg, Monyash, Bakewell), 192 (Buxton, Chelmorton, Monyash, Buxton) and 446 (Leek, Longnor, Hartington, Bakewell).

OVERVIEW/INTEREST

Pleasant, open, rural landscapes to start with.

Section along High Peak and Tissington Trails.

Fantastic limestone scenery of Biggin Dale, Mill Dale and Dove Dale.

Cliffs, tors, towers, rocks, screes, caves and stepping stones in abundance.

Tranquil woodlands lining the meandering River Dove.

Superb scenery throughout the stage.

FOOTPATHS/WAYSIGNS

For much of the way, particularly along the Trails and in Dove Dale, the paths and, where needed, the signposting is very good indeed.

The in-between bits are more complicated and you will need to follow carefully the directions given.

There are some minor waterlogged areas on the connecting cross-country sections and in the lower reaches of Biggin Dale but nothing to test your avoidance skills severely.

Virtually no erosion anywhere.

OVERALL TIME ALLOWANCE 6½ hours

Statistics		
Distance walked	**Km**	**Miles**
	21.4	13.3
Height climbed	**M**	**Feet**
	150	490
Principal heights	**M**	**Feet**
Monyash	270	885
Thorpe Cloud (if climbed)	287	940

The way to Heathcote (Allow 2 hours)

From the village green in the centre of Monyash, select the minor lane signed to 'Newhaven 4 – Youlgreave 6 – White Peak Scenic Route' and walk S along Rakes Road. As you walk away from the village, wander over to the low walling on your L for a really attractive view across the pond to the spired village church surrounded by a cluster of stone houses. Pass by Rake End Farm and follow the road as it bends round sharply to the R. You will then be walking SW uphill into a tree-lined, rural landscape of orderly fields bounded by limestone walling.

Towards the top of the brow you walk beneath a three-stranded electricity line and from here on the views become wide vistas of flattish, green countryside dotted with sheep. The next important landmark is the entrance track to Highlow Farm which is passed to your R. About 200 paces after this, turn off R along a signed public footpath and continue SW. Cross a low stile in a stone wall and, main-

5:1 *Departing from Monyash on a crisp, sunny morning*

taining your SW diagonal, cross the next limestone wall through a gap and then veer R proceeding WSW to locate and use another low stile in the wall directly ahead. Cross the adjacent meadow on your established diagonal to reach a G-stile near the corner of the field. This stile is to the L of a post supporting telephone wires. Pass beneath these cables and then bear slightly L to pass through another G-stile to the L of two trees. Cross the next field on a similar SW diagonal to reach the main A515 road at MR 144643, accessed by a stile to the R of a metal gate.

Cross this busy road with great care. Within 50 paces, escape from the road by turning R over an S-stile to reach a public footpath commencing at the corner of a field. The path leads SW to pass round to the L of Moscar Farm. This can be a muddy passage as the farm entrance is often churned up by the hooves of cattle. Watch out for electric fences in this vicinity. Cross the farm approach lane and then cross the retaining wall on the far side by means of an S-stile near a public footpath sign. Then bear R to exit from the enclosed compound through a metal gate, where it is usually muddy. Continue downhill next to a stone wall on your R across grassy, well-drained slopes. Wide landscapes of rounded, green hills appear ahead. The route continues downhill over two more S-stiles to reach the High Peak Trail at MR 143639.

Turn L along the Trail to continue, initially E but soon veering S as the embankment curves to your R along a bend which was designed

5:2 *The scar of Long Dale seen from the Tissington Trail*

for trains. From here, navigation for some distance is straightforward and you may concentrate your full attention on the views. Walking is now along a wide, well-drained, level, elevated track where you can achieve fast progress southwards. Your long strides may, however, be interrupted by the picnic area, toilets, and café at Parsley Hay. It would be cheating to hire any of the bikes invitingly stacked here! Continue s along the Trail, passing over a bridge across a road, before reaching the junction which signifies the commencement of the Tissington Trail at MR 147633. Bear R along this.

Your slightly changed direction is now ssw as you walk into a deep cutting through the hillside ahead. This is surrounded by the Parsley Hay Nature Reserve administered by the Derbyshire Wildlife Trust. You are requested not to damage the Reserve or disturb the wildlife. Out of the cutting, the Trail passes beneath an arched stone bridge and then the embankment leads you round a broad curve to the R where there are views to the w, including glimpses of a deep, narrow, irregular cleft. This is the outline of Long Dale. The extensive barns, outbuildings and used rubber tyres of Hartington Moor Farm are quickly left behind down to your R. A short distance further s along the Trail, another shallow cutting is entered, this one containing particularly absorbing exposed limestone and sandstone bedding planes. The way then passes high above the B5054 road linking Newhaven and Hartington, by means of a bridge with exceptionally high retaining walls.

The next significant feature is the disused signal box at the former Hartington Station with its signals permanently set so as not to delay your progress. In addition to a large car park, there is a delightful picnic area and toilets. Just beyond the signal box it is necessary to leave the Trail by turning off along the waysigned (No. 2) footpath on your R that leads to Heathcote. The narrow path winds SW, initially between subtantial retaining walls.

There are stiles along here, the first being a wooden step one. Keep next to a dry-stone wall on your L when more open terrain is reached to pass by a wooden bench near a gap in a stone wall ahead. Still keeping beside the wall, pass through a narrow G-stile to the L of a wooden gate and then maintain a SW bearing along the edge of the next field to pass through a similar stile. Another one follows, the narrow gap of this one needlessly obstructed by the protruding bars of a metal gate. From here, a better-defined walled track leads to White House Farm following a kink to the L. Turn L along the lane ahead and walk SSE to reach the junction of roads at Heathcote. This is at MR 146603.

The way to Milldale *(Allow 2½ hours)*

Continue straight across the junction walking SSE to pass Glebe House Farm (where bed-and-breakfast may be obtained). A short distance further on, before coming to a stone building with distinctive lancet windows, turn down the next public footpath leading off on the R. The route passes through Chapel Farm. At the far end, bear R to cross the adjacent field in line with an important S-stile, to the L of a metal gate, over the stone wall ahead; the approach to this stile is to the SW. Beware of an unexpectedly steep drop on the far side! Then head downhill towards a lane at a point where a walled track down the far hillside converges. You may see donkeys on the slopes you are now crossing. Over the S-stile at the bottom of the hill, turn L and SE along the narrow lane. (The National Park Rangers point out that this lane has no verges and is quite busy! They suggest this stretch can be avoided by making use of the side lane tracking uphill to the SW before turning SE to reach Biggin Dale via a bridleway.) Follow the narrow lane as far as Dale End at MR 147596. The road divides just beyond the buildings and at this point branch off down the public footpath on the R, passing through a G-stile at a wooden gate.

You are now in position to enter Biggin Dale at English Nature's National Nature Reserve and a sign to your L welcomes you to do this. A wide, partially grassed-over track winds downhill into the recesses of the dale, the sides of which progressively steepen and deepen as a tiny water treatment plant (named a 'Sewage Works' on the OLM) is passed to your R. The remoteness of the dale intensifies as it curves round to the L, with springy turf underfoot. Beyond the next P-and

5:3 *Sticks and stones in Biggin Dale*

W-stile, keep straight ahead along the dale when you come to an intersection of ways, passing a sign reading 'Public Bridleway to Biggin Dale'. The correct path then leads round to the L along the floor of the dale and through a swing gate. It passes round a concrete watering hole for animals to your R to continue SW as a bridleway down Biggin Dale. This is from MR 145588. It can be extremely muddy in this vicinity and in the next section.

The continuation way follows the course of a dry-stone wall, keeping to the L of this. Gorse bushes, scree and limestone outcrops begin to appear. Along here, keep always to the bottom of the cleft, ignoring all footpaths leading out of the dale to either L or R. Go through a swing gate and past a National Trust sign. Trees and bushes appear for the first time (mainly hawthorn and beech) and quite suddenly a new watercourse pops up from underground to your L. This signals the end of the relatively dry part of the dale. Through the next gateway, the going underfoot becomes appreciably more rocky and for some distance this rougher ground has to be shared with the stream, which increases in volume from the contributions of several feeder channels. The spectacular limestone tors now in view high above on your R are quite magnificent. This superb scenery is with you for the rest of the short remaining distance into the valley connecting Wolfscote Dale and Mill Dale at the confluence with Biggin Dale. This meeting place is marked by a breathtaking array of exposed limestone ridges, pikes and columns. This delightful spot is at MR 142569.

Turn L along the excellent path leading southwards which follows the meanders of the wide and powerful River Dove. You immediately pass through a narrow G-stile before crossing a short causeway. Progress from here is to the SE along an even more spectacular dale through which the river is gouging an ever-deepening channel. Iron Tors cave is passed, above on your L; a narrow path leads to it. Apart from minor obstacles, such as stiles, progress downstream along the banks of the River Dove is uneventful. However, do not cross the river when you come to a wooden footbridge in the vicinity of an unoccupied stone building. After reaching a narrow G-stile at a gate, pass a series of gorse-covered slopes and ignore another footbridge across the Dove. Instead, continue through another G-stile and on down the dale. This scenery continues until the dale and river bend round more abruptly to the L.

At a twin G-stile, the National Trust ground of Fishpond Bank is reached. This is a really delightful spot with an arched stone road bridge spanning the River Dove. The wooded slopes of Lode Plantation rise across the river to your R and the rocky spur ahead is that of Shining Tor. Climb the stone steps and use the bridge to cross the river. On the far side, immediately branch L to walk along the lane where restrictions are imposed on vehicular traffic but not on walkers. Continue W to reach the tiny hamlet of Milldale less than 1 km (about ½ mile) further on. Make use of the footpath looping off to your L during your approach to Milldale to escape wherever possible from walking along the surfaced lane. Cross the river again here by means of the double-arched, narrow stone bridge (Viator's Bridge), bearing L to do so. You could visit the National Trust Information Barn, refreshment shop and toilet facilities.

The way to Ilam/Thorpe (Allow 2 hours)

From the hamlet of Milldale, continue S along the public footpath leading towards Dove Dale, passing through a swing gate in the process. In spite of a succession of gates and S-stiles, you can make rapid progress down the dale along an excellent renovated path. Keep to the obvious main path along the bottom of the dale avoiding all side paths including one signed to 'Alsop-en-le-Dale 1¾'. More impressive limestone features appear, including large caves up to your L (Dove Holes), before the steep-sided valley of Hall Dale appears across the river leading off to the W. This is another dry dale and climbing up it is one of the suggested extensions. The way to it is across the next footbridge, which should be ignored by those following the main route. The bridge is near some spectacular limestone columns, including Ilam Rock and Pickering Tor, and there are more large caves. The steep slopes are thickly wooded: the far steep banks are Hurt's Wood, with Upper Taylor's Wood on your side of the river.

Next a spectacular gorge is entered and progress through here is on elevated wooden duck-boards. Quite often these are only just above the torrents that rush through the narrow opening about half a metre (1-2 ft) on your R. Exercise caution here as the boards can become slippery when wet and there is a constant two-way flow of walkers through the gorge so that somebody has to pass on the outside!

A succession of stunning features now follow as you continue southwards along Dove Dale. These, in approach sequence, include the Natural Arch (a huge rock archway above on your L), Jacob's Ladder (up a limestone cliff on far side of river), Tissington Spires (jagged, tooth-like limestone columns rearing above to your L; for experienced climbers only) and The Twelve Apostles. These latter limestone tors are on the far side of the river opposite Lover's Leap, a craggy promontory towering above the river just off to the R. The path climbs up to Lover's Leap, the highest point reached. The inclines to get there and back down to the river level have recently been further improved and the Leap is now reached and left along comfortable stepped tiers. Be very careful if you decide to peer over the edge because the well-worn limestone rocks overlooking the sheer drop are slippery, even when completely dry.

5:4 *Tissington Spires, Dove Dale*

5:5 *Looking along Dove Dale towards Twelve Apostles*

Beyond these features the dale winds further southwards to the entrance to Lin Dale, a green valley rising to the SE, off on the L. Between this and the continuation of Dove Dale is the pointed peak of Thorpe Cloud rising steeply to a height of 287 m (940 ft) and climbed as one of the suggested extensions. Pass through one of twin G-stiles near a gateway at the entrance to Lin Dale at MR 151514. Thereafter, several choices are possible.

If you are making for accommodation at Thorpe, the best route is to turn L along Lin Dale and walk up the grassy valley as far as the col at the head of the dale. Swing R to pass Hamston Hill on your L and then choose one of the footpaths leading S into the village of Thorpe.

If your overnight stay is in Ilam, continue S down Dove Dale. There are two other ways of reaching this village. If the stepping stones opposite the entrance to Hall Dale are above water, you can cross the river by them and then continue downstream along the W bank of the Dove. Should these stones be submerged, continue downstream on the L bank of the river until you can cross it over a footbridge. Either alternative takes you past the extensive car parking area, toilets and café at MR 146509. Opposite these facilities, there is a footpath leading off W and above the Izaak Walton Hotel which will take you into Ilam about 1 km (about ½ mile) away. However, this path becomes extremely muddy in wet weather. In such conditions, continue further S down the lane before turning R along the minor road leading W into Ilam.

Alternatives

EXTENSIONS

You can also walk the length of Hall Dale. This is best achieved by departing from the main route at Milldale (MR 139547) by turning R and W up the minor lane. Turn off L along the next footpath and follow this towards Stanshope. Just before you reach Stanshope, turn L again to connect with the footpaths that will lead you into Hall Dale. It is a superb descent under towering, scree-lined slopes along a grass and stone track. This way down is a bit slippery in places so watch your step along here! When you reach Dove Dale, turn R and walk S until you reach the footbridge below Ilam Rock. Cross the River Dove here to return to the main route at MR 142531.

Another extension is to climb to the top of Thorpe Cloud. From MR 151514 at the entrance to Lin Dale there is an obvious narrow path which snakes up the face of the hill across several craggy limestone outcrops; all you need is sure footing and a head for heights. The views from the top are terrific but make sure your footholds are sound because the summit rocks are smooth and slippery and the wind can gust alarmingly round this exposed position. There is an alternative path down which weaves round the SE slopes of the hill to reach a trough at the bottom of the steeper section. Turn R here and a track will lead you westwards back into Dove Dale, avoiding ground which is currently closed due to renovation work.

EASIER ROUTES

This stage is very direct with interesting scenery throughout and there are no steep hills to climb. No easier routes are offered.

5:6 *Eventide at Dove Dale*

Stage 6

ILAM/THORPE TO LONGNOR

*6 Looking north-west across the Manifold Valley
near Castern Hall*

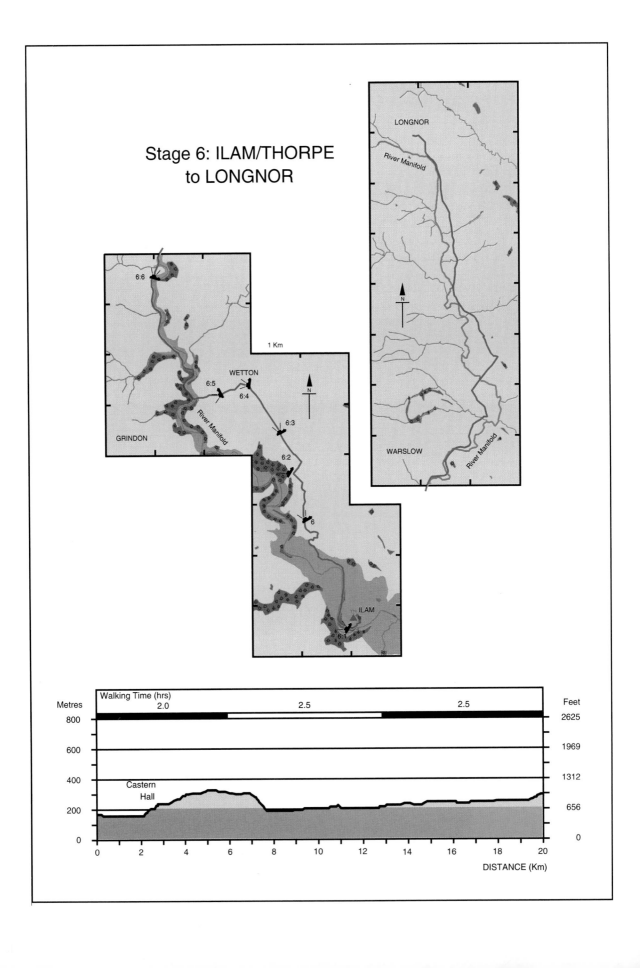

Stage 6: ILAM/THORPE to LONGNOR

LONGNOR

River Manifold

N

WARSLOW

River Manifold

6:6

WETTON

6:5

6:4

6:3

6:2

GRINDON

River Manifold

6

1 Km

N

ILAM

6:1

Walking Time (hrs)

Metres

2.0   2.5   2.5

Feet

800   2625

600   1969

400   1312

Castern
Hall

200   656

0   0

0   2   4   6   8   10   12   14   16   18   20

DISTANCE (Km)

STARTING LOCATION
Ilam Hall to the sw of Ilam Village at the
    southern tip of Dove Dale.
OLM 24/MR 131506
Good car parking facilities at Ilam Hall.
Directions start from Ilam Hall.

PUBLIC TRANSPORT
Bus routes 57A, 202 (Mansfield, Derby,
    Hartington, Castleton), 443 (Ashbourne,
    Mapleton, Thorpe, Ilam) and 450
    (Milldale, Alstonefield, Ilam, Leek).

OVERVIEW/INTEREST
Ilam Hall church (St Bertram's Chapel),
    parkland and gardens.
Spectacular start along and above the
    Manifold Valley.
Castern Hall and village of Wetton visited.
Precipitous cliff with Thor's Cave.
Section along Manifold Way passing
    Wettonmill and walking through tunnel
    near Swainsley.
Radcliffe's Folly below Ecton Hill.
Approach to Longnor up wide valley with
    rural landscapes.
Attractive scenery and plenty of interest
    throughout walk.

FOOTPATHS/WAYSIGNS
Footpaths and signs are something of a mixture.

In the Manifold Valley and along the
    Manifold Way the dry paths are very good;
    however, the Way has to be shared with
    numerous cyclists, some moving fast, so
    watch out!
In between, the signs are fairly adequate but
    not over-generous; consequently, there
    are a few points where route finding is a
    challenge.
In the rural areas during wet weather, there
    are numerous muddy patches and places
    where surface water holds. This is particu-
    larly onerous when approaching farms:
    ground near gate entrances is often
    churned up by cattle. Plenty of very
    narrow G-stiles along the way.

OVERALL TIME ALLOWANCE 7 hours

Statistics		
Distance walked	**Km**	**Miles**
	20.1	12.5
Height climbed	**M**	**Feet**
	330	1080
Principal heights	**M**	**Feet**
Tumulus at MR 117541	328	1075
(SE of Wetton)		
Ecton Hill (if visited)	369	1210

The way to Wetton *(Allow 2 hours)*

From either Thorpe or Ilam, make your way to Ilam Hall, just to the
sw of Ilam Village. It is approached through immaculate parklands
that contain many specimen trees. The Hall is a splendid building with
turrets, castellated walling, arched doorways and the most unusual
fluted chimneys. If you are walking there from Thorpe, use the connecting narrow roads leading w as this will get you into position to
commence the described Stage 6 as quickly as possible, rather than
following the more complicated and hilly way there by footpath. At
the Hall there is a YH and also a National Trust Information Centre,
shop and tea room.

Walk through the car parking area in front of the buildings and turn R through the terraced gardens following the signs directing you towards the Manifold Tea Rooms. These you pass on your R. Then turn L, away from the buildings, and follow the zigzag path down the flights of steps to reach the River Manifold, flowing along the valley below. Turn R to walk westwards along the valley floor. Steep, wooded slopes line the valley at this point providing an atmosphere of comfortable seclusion. The secure, dry, flat compacted path leads past the shaft of a stone cross. This was extracted from the foundations of a cottage during the rebuilding of Ilam in 1840 and is traditionally known as the 'Battle Stone', being associated with a struggle between the Saxons and Danes in the middle of the eleventh century.

The valley then narrows appreciably and its flanks progressively decline in height as you continue upstream. In this section, ignore a stile and footpath leading off to the L. More open landscapes are entered and there are extensive views of low green hills and fertile grazing slopes. A stile and wooden fence mark the boundary of the enclosed woodlands and pastures of Ilam Country Park protected by the National Trust.

Continue upstream, forsaking a footbridge across the river for the opportunity to pass through an unusual iron G-stile at an iron gate. The way continues northwards from here, always close to the banks of the River Manifold. After crossing another wooden S-stile, the obvious route along the river leads to River Lodge, built in 1840. This is reached at MR 129518. Having passed through the stile and iron gate at the cottage, bear L along the macadam lane to progress NW further up the valley. Cross a cattle grid and select the R-hand fork when the lane divides, to pass a small grass triangle to your L. (The restrictive

6:1 *The lush foliage lining the River Manifold below Ilam Hall* sign here does not apply to walkers unless they intend to park.) Pleasant farmlands stretch ahead and up the slopes on your R along the now quite wide and shallow valley. Keep to the farm road as it twists up the slopes ahead. There are a number of marginal short-cuts along the alternative diagonal tracks to the R but these are up steep, grassy slopes and they tend to become slippery when wet. During this ascent there are good views of Bunster Hill, back down the valley to the E and these provide a good excuse to pause for breath.

Higher up, the surfaced lane passes through a gateway in a stone wall and then it leads to the R, round the imposing buildings of Castern Hall, the enclosed grounds of which are well protected by high railings. The way round is indicated by a footpath sign (arrow-head). Cross over a cattle grid and continue slightly uphill along the winding lane. At the next bend, veer off to the L to follow a public footpath signed to 'Wetton'. Next, use the stile or wooden gate to access a broad track with a grass-covered centre which leads NW. You are now walking well above the Manifold Valley and there are extensive views down into it, over on your L. Beyond a G-stile at a wooden gate, the correct continuation way becomes somewhat less well defined. However, press on confidently by bearing to the R up a gentle, grassy slope. Pass through another G-stile at a gate ahead and then veer further R still, gaining height as you walk along a broad, grassy diagonal which kinks to the L further up the gentle slopes. There are superb

6:2 *The view northwards along the Manifold Valley, taking in Beeston Tor*

open views along here down to your L back into the valley. The suggested way then curves to reach another G-stile, this one to the L of a wooden gate. After this, walk northwards along the edge of the adjacent field following the line of a dry-stone wall immediately on your R. The way then passes through a gap at the termination of another stone wall ahead. As you continue N from this elevated crossing, the jagged scar of Dove Dale may be observed across open country over to your R, to the E. Having crossed the next field you will reach, at another G-stile and gate, a well-signed intersection of ways which fan out in several directions. These include your own exacting approach route from Castern Hall and ways to Ilam via Damgate, to Hopedale and towards Wetton. The latter, a L turn along a walled lane, is your continuation route. Walk NW along the narrow walled lane, sections of which become very muddy in winter. It leads towards a rounded hillock ahead and passes to the R of a tumulus. There are more fine, open views along the approach to this including a sighting of the village of Alstonefield, across country on your R, to the NE. Over the brow of the hill, the church and houses of the village of Wetton first come into view directly ahead. To the R and beyond the village are the pointed tumuli to the E of Wetton Hill, the highest points in the immediate area to the N of the village. The lane drops down the hillside and, after crossing a minor junction, continues NW to pass the hill of Wetton Low (another tumulus), the trig point of which may be observed above to your L. When you reach Wetton, avoid turning either L or R but instead head uphill towards the church and the centre of the tiny village at Ye Olde Royal Oak Inn.

The way to Hulme End *(Allow 2½ hours)*

Depart from Wetton along the path leading W through the cemetery. This is signed to 'Wetton Mill 1½ (Manifold Valley) – Butterton 2½' and the churchyard is entered and left through K-gates. Turn L along the road when you reach the church schoolhouse, to walk WSW away from the village, passing Carr Farms and Newhouse. Bear R at the T-junction ahead, along the road again signed to 'Wetton Mill and Butterton', walking slightly downhill. Be careful to pass by a narrow lane to your L but immediately after turn L through a G-stile in a stone wall to continue along a footpath signed to 'Thor's Cave ½ Mile.' It can be extremely muddy in the adjacent field, which you have to find your way across. Then a narrow path leads downhill across firmer ground towards the jaws of the deepening side dale and the wider Manifold Valley to the W. The steep limestone cliffs ahead on the L

6:3 Reflections on the way to Wetton

Above: 6:4 *The way leads right through Wetton churchyard*

contain Thor's Cave, a large cavern with abandoned rock-climbing equipment still fixed to its roof.

After you have passed through a metal gate, the rate of descent increases as the grassy side slopes funnel into a narrower and steeper cleft ahead. Make for the G-stile below (during your approach to this, the entrance to Thor's Cave can be seen). A rough path, often muddy, leads steeply down from the stile, between hawthorn and other shrubs. Near the bottom of the slope and just after passing through another G-stile, a path to the L leads up to Thor's Cave. (You are recommended to visit this interesting feature if you are happy about the climb, but note that you will have to retrace your steps down into the Manifold Valley afterwards.) The main route then leads across the footbridge over the River Manifold. This is at MR 099551. Turn R on the far side to continue northwards along the winding valley by means of the Manifold Way – a wide ribbon of macadam shared with cyclists. Do be aware of the presence of these riders, particularly those silently overtaking from your rear.

A short distance further on, a giant limestone tor looms up ahead and the way curves in its shadow. There are limestone hills on the far side of the valley. Glance to your R rear and take a final look back towards the black hole of Thor's Cave. Cross the river by a substantial bridge and immediately fork L along the lane nearest to the river, heading towards another impressive limestone outcrop. The river is

Right: 6:5 *The descent to the Manifold Valley at Thor's Cave*

then crossed again at an arched stone bridge named Dafar Bridge. You next reach a ford across a fast-flowing tributary of the River Manifold; when this is in flood, work your way round to the L by using the footbridge to cross it. Wettonmill is just over the river here and a modest diversion will take you there, perhaps to sample the delicious coffee which is served in the Mill café. Toilets are also available and these are at MR 096561.

Continue northwards along the Manifold Way on the w bank of the river. The next section makes use of a minor road for about 2 km (1¼ miles) and during this stretch the valley becomes progressively less rugged as the limestone tors and cliffs give way to more gentle, tree-covered slopes of only modest height. This transition intensifies as the valley widens and the less steep slopes become covered with grass and sheep. Another tributary stream is crossed and then the dominant escarpment of Ecton Hill comes into view on the far side of the river. The next interesting feature is passing through a long, narrow tunnel near Swainsley. This underground passage is illuminated but do take heed of passing motorists who may be surprised at your presence in it. When necessary, quickly duck out of their way by slipping into one of the V-shaped spaces in the side walls. Emerging into daylight once more, cross the road and walk along the continuation of the Manifold Way northwards up the valley. Progress along the valley is uneventful until you see some unusual green-painted spires on a large building across the water. These are at Ecton and belong to Radcliffe's Folly. On the steep hillsides above this frivolity there is

6:6 The tunnel near Ecton Bridge with one of the passing alcoves in the side exposed

evidence of a massive landslip and this is perhaps of more pertinent interest to walkers.

The main stream is recrossed at a point where the houses of Ecton are tiered on the slopes to your R, rising towards the folly. Cross the roadway at the gates ahead to continue up the now quite shallow, valley. About 1 km (½ mile) further NE, the Manifold Way ends rather abruptly at Hulme End.

In your approach to Hulme End keep to the Manifold Way right to its termination at an extensive car-parking area. This involves crossing the river again and avoiding all side paths. Once past the car-parking area, bear R before crossing the B5054 road and then turn L along the minor side road, walking round a derelict building. This is at MR 104593.

The way to Longnor *(Allow 2½ hours)*

After the lane bends progressively to your L, select the public footpath leading off to the R. This is accessed at a wooden stile in a hawthorn hedge. Bear L from here to walk diagonally NNW across the field, using a W-stile to gain entrance to the next, enclosed field. From here, the twin peaks of Chrome Hill and Parkhouse Hill may be observed as tiny pimples on the distant horizon to the N. Cross the (often muddy) cattle entrance to a gateway, proceed through the G-stile straight ahead and then turn sharp R to cross a wooden fence at an S-stile beside a cattle drinking trough. Continue downhill to the NE as indicated by the foot-path sign, heading directly in line with Lowend Farm (near Townend) which is part way up the hillside across the River Manifold. At the bottom of the brow an often exacting muddy area has to be crossed. In your approach to this, veer R round the rough, steep, final drop, before turning L to locate and use a critical narrow G-stile in a stone wall ahead. There is usually a mire on the far side which you will have to edge round cautiously.

A grassy track then leads fairly directly to a narrow-railed footbridge across the River Manifold at MR 102601. Continue heading NE, now up gentle, dry slopes, to reach and pass through a G-stile in a stone wall above. Lowend Farm is then passed over to your R as the path winds further uphill beside a fence and intermittent hedge on your L. On the way up, turn round to observe the far-ranging views domin-ated by Ecton Hill, now appearing to the S. Towards the top of the field, turn sharp L to pass through a G-stile between two metal gates in order to continue northwards up the valley along the waysigned (yellow arrowheads) path. Go through another G-stile to the L of a wooden gate immediately ahead. Beyond this, an elevated way leads northwards beside a stone wall to the R; the River Manifold is now some distance below to the W. Beyond a boarded-up stone building the way passes through a gap in the stone wall ahead. An awkward

W-stile has to be negotiated and, after crossing a muddy dip, the way rises up a more agreeable grassy brow.

Another G-stile, adjacent to a wooden gate, leads to a narrow back lane along which you bear L to head NNW. The continuation way is through the farmlands which occupy the wide, shallow upper reaches of the Manifold Valley. The lane leads into the cluster of buildings at Brund where you should ignore a footpath veering off uphill to your R. Instead, follow the signed public footpath on your L and drop down the adjacent field to reach a G-stile in the wall at the bottom, carefully crossing (or veering round to the R of) a fast-flowing, small stream in the process. Turn R up the narrow lane; as it starts to bend L, select the narrow footpath on the L signed to 'Longnor'. After passing through a short, enclosed section, use the S-stile in a stone wall to enter more open country. Continue heading NW from here, initially following the line of a dilapidated stone wall. Across the next field, the way leads between wire fences at a point where the river comes temporarily into view down on your L and where you have to contend with more mud in wet conditions.

Keep heading northwards, eventually passing a waysign which provides early warning of another crucial stile 40 paces ahead. (You will understand better just how helpful this sign is when you reach the spot!) Use this narrow G-stile to get across the stone wall to your L. Your N bearing is then maintained by continuing to head up the valley beside a fenced-off area of scrub, above on your R. This relatively complicated part of the way then leads to a wooden S-stile and over this you are briefly connected with the river once more. Walk up the narrow path ahead in the direction indicated by the white arrowhead. Another combination of a muddy crossing with drier slopes beyond lies ahead. This is followed by a diagonal approach to another G-stile where again the continuation way is helpfully signed. Many more stiles, fields (often muddy), and the crossing of several brooks follow as you continue northwards along the valley, passing round several farms and residences, including those at Pool, Ridge End Farm and Lower Boothlow, all shown on the OLM. Along this testing stretch always keep to the path and signed way leading N and avoid the occasional side path and the stiles which will divert you to either W or E. There is also one division in the main path and when you reach this, veer L along the lower way nearest to the river. The correct route becomes better defined as you progress up the valley and this is indicated by a combination of yellow and white arrowheads and daubings of white paint on the stonework and at stiles. In particular, the accepted ways round the farms are marked where this is considered necessary. Watch out for barbed wire at a couple of the stiles, one of which is partly concealed by a vastly overgrown hawthorn hedge.

Eventually you will approach the village of Longnor, its buildings visible on the skyline above on your R. In the vicinity of MR 092645, prepare to head to the R up the slopes away from the river. There is no clear path here and in winter the ground is often wet and muddy. Look out for the spot where the river twists to form a small but distinct oxbow lake: opposite this point veer R to walk N, diagonally away from the river. The correct direction is in line with the church tower visible above the trees ahead. This will lead you to a G-stile in the stone wall above and it is essential that you pass through it. This critical stile is about 100 paces away from a white-painted metal gate which must not be used!

Now head up the slope leading to the R of Folds End farm above, choosing a diagonal approach line and making for the upper L-hand corner of the field, following only the faintest of paths. Pass over the W-stile and head directly towards the outbuildings of the farm, then pass between the shippens. Climb over another W-stile at the buildings where a sign reads 'Single File Please'. Continue through the immaculately kept farmyard, bearing R, and then use the farm entrance lane to reach the road above. Turn L for the short remaining distance into the centre of Longnor. In the village, there is a good choice of hostelries.

Alternatives

EXTENSIONS

Although this stage is not particularly strenuous in physical terms, route finding is challenging at times and you will do well if you manage to keep to the way already described.

In addition to the short exploration of Thor's Cave mentioned in the description of the main route (p.103), another rewarding extension is to climb to the top of Ecton Hill for outstanding views overlooking the twisting Manifold Valley. To get there, depart from the main route at Wettonmill and follow the footpaths leading N through Dale Farm and round the rocky outcrop of Sugarloaf to reach Broad Ecton Farm. Turn R before reaching these farm buildings. From here, relatively obvious paths will guide you to the summit of Ecton Hill at 369 m (1210 ft). Good paths then lead further northwards from the summit, along the spur of the ridge and down into Ecton where the main route may be rejoined after crossing the River Manifold at Dale Bridge (MR 095584).

EASIER ROUTES

The main route, although relatively complicated, is one of the most direct walking routes between Ilam and Longnor. There is no better or more interesting walking alternative which appreciably shortens the main route. Should significant problems arise or be anticipated, the stage could be divided by staying overnight at one of the small intervening villages such as Grindon, Wetton, Butterton or Warslow.

Stage 7

LONGNOR TO TIDESWELL

7 *The gentle approach to bisect Aldery Cliff and High Wheeldon*

Stage 7: LONGNOR to TIDESWELL

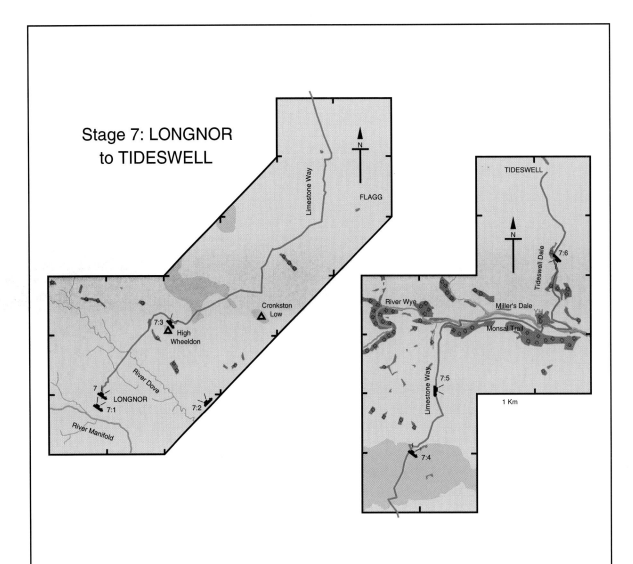

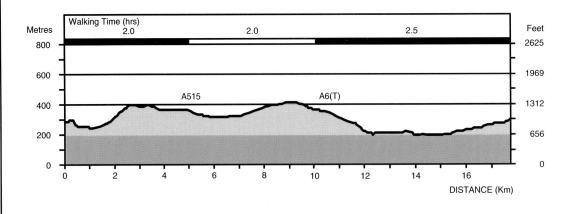

STARTING LOCATION

The village of Longnor on the B5053 road, about 9 km (5½ miles) SSE of Buxton. OLM 24/MR 089649.

Small car parking area in front of Market Hall; holds no more than about 10 vehicles. Directions start from centre of village.

PUBLIC TRANSPORT

Bus routes 442 (Ashbourne, Hartington, Longnor, Buxton), 445 (Leek, Warslow, Longnor), 446 (Leek, Longnor, Hartington, Bakewell), 456 (Hartington, Longnor, Butterton, Leek), 460 (Flash, Longnor, Warslow) and 464 (Hanley, Leek, Hartington, Longnor).

OVERVIEW/INTEREST

Varied route across open country and along confined dales.

Interesting views and features throughout, including limestone outcrops.

Crossing upper reaches of River Dove; observations of climbers on rock faces at Aldery Cliff.

Sections along Limestone Way and Monsal Trail.

Spectacular finish from Miller's Dale up Tideswell Dale.

FOOTPATHS/WAYSIGNS

For the most part, the paths and signs are reasonable to very good.

Noticeable absence of rough ground and minimum waterlogged areas.

Several stretches along back-lanes and walled tracks where fast, unhindered progress is possible.

Relatively few stiles to cross but some of these are awkward and not all that obvious to locate. A few are in need of urgent renovation.

Overall route finding should present few significant challenges.

OVERALL TIME ALLOWANCE   6½ hours

Statistics		
Distance walked	**Km**	**Miles**
	17.7	11
Height climbed	**M**	**Feet**
	410	1345
Principal heights	**M**	**Feet**
Taddington Moor	420	1380

The way to the A515 at Pomeroy *(Allow 2 hours)*

From the centre of the village, near the ancient Toll Market, select the minor lane by the side of the Grapes Inn to walk NE, passing by the churchyard to your L. Cross the road ahead on a diagonal to the L and within a few paces walk up the signed public footpath off to the R. This leads gently uphill along a shallow gully which threads between earth embankments. The direction is N. An open gateway is reached: pass through the gap to the R of this. Bear R across the adjacent field, changing your direction to NE, and over the brow of the slope ahead there is a recently renovated stile in the hawthorn hedge directly in front of you. There are superb views from here, into and across the wide valley of the Dove. Directly below, but still some distance away, are the hills of Aldery Cliff and High Wheeldon, with your continuation route threading a way between them. To your L, and further away, lie Chrome Hill and Parkhouse Hill, jutting up to the NW, whilst to your R the views are towards Crowdecote and down the valley to the SE.

From your elevated viewing position follow the broad, grassy track down into the valley. This starts to the L and then zigzags down the steep slope towards the stone barn directly below. Part of the way down becomes rather slippery with mud in wet weather. Walk round the barn by turning first L and then almost immediately R along the signed public footpath. This is accessed by means of a metal gate. The way then leads NE across meadowlands. These are often churned up by cattle in winter and in such conditions the best way round the worst of the mud is usually next to the stone wall on the R. In making this detour, be careful not to tangle with dangerously close barbed wire! Head directly towards the gap in the hills you are approaching, walking up a slight incline and maintaining your NE bearing. Over the brow, a better defined way leads down across grassy slopes to reach and cross the infant River Dove by Beggar's Bridge at MR 094657.

Left: 7:1 *The plaque says it all!*

Below: 7:2 *The view northwards from near Crowdecote towards Chrome and Parkhouse Hills*

An obvious path leads from the river beside a hawthorn hedge to connect (after passing over a stile) with the track to Underhill Farm. At this stile be careful not to follow a path leading off over a stone wall on your R. Bear R along the surfaced lane to reach a minor road ahead, along which you turn L. This junction is reached at MR 097661. Walk up the road northwards to pass by the interesting rock faces of the disused quarry gouged from Aldery Cliff. (This is owned by the British Mountaineering Council, its only such possession, and was sold to them by an entrepreneur who tells me he has retained wood-gathering rights on the land! There are some severe rock climbing routes up these almost vertical cliffs.) Turn R opposite the quarry and use a wooden stile to gain entry to a narrow, grassy waymarked path which leads E across the National Trust ground of High Wheeldon.

The way is then up a narrow side dale that contains modest outcrops of limestone, with glimpses of steep, craggy slopes on your R. More height is quickly gained along the grassy dale and the views to the rear improve as you go up. Then a more comfortable shallow gradient is reached as the surrounding slopes level off towards the top of the dale, which begins to peter out. When you reach the next National Trust sign, turn L over the wooden waymarked stile to cross the dip ahead and arrive at a minor road (MR 103662). (The rising path on the R at the turning leads to the top of High Wheeldon and the minor diversion to get there is suggested as one of the lesser extensions, see p.121.) Enter the lane leading to Wheeldon Trees Farm by a metal gate, turn L and then immediately R along the narrow road. Within a further 25 paces bear off L up the surfaced track, which initially leads ESE. The way then bends progressively to the L to reach Hurdlow Grange and Hall, about 1 km (about ½ mile) away. Open views abound in all directions during your approach to these buildings. Keep to the main track now leading eastwards, bypassing a grassy, walled track to your L and then a signed path also leading off that way. Just before reaching the Grange and Hall, a disused, former single-track branch railway line is crossed, where the remains of the curved embankment are still visible to your R.

Turn L opposite the first buildings and climb over the stepped W-stile to follow the waysigned public footpath leading towards Pomeroy and Flagg. (The wall here is liberally daubed with yellow paint.) Continue northwards across the adjacent field to climb another S-stile to the R of a metal gate in the wall ahead. Then continue walking N across grassy slopes, by the side of a limestone wall on your L, to reach the main A515 road. This connection is made at Street Farm, Pomeroy, opposite the Duke of York Inn (MR 119674) and you will have crossed the High Peak Trail in getting there. The approach to the Trail is a bit complicated. Another stone wall has to be crossed by

7:3 *The continuation route observed from a snow-covered High Wheeldon*

means of an S-stile which necessitates an awkward step down; a second wall is crossed by a wooden-framed S-stile, before you veer R through a metal gate to cross the dell ahead and then the High Peak Trail, the latter by an impressively wide, arched stone bridge. Another metal gate on the far side of the bridge provides entrance to a diagonal way to the L which will lead you to your rendezvous with the A515 road.

The way to the A6(T) road at the Waterloo Inn
(Allow 2 hours)

Cross the busy A515 road with care, selecting a diagonal to your R. Almost immediately, turn off to the L along the continuation footpath to resume your predominant NE direction of travel through these parts. This bearing leads through a gap in the stone wall ahead, after which you bear L to reach a strategic, venerable S-stile, roughly midway along the limestone wall ahead. The wording 'Pasture Barn' appearing on your OLM can be quite misleading: the name relates to a collection of sheep pens, not a barn. On the far side of the stile, be careful to track NE – use your compass here to confirm the direction because it is that important! Head for the far corner wall of the next field and use twin W-stiles (ancient and badly in need of attention) to cross first the corner walling and then another wall immediately ahead on your L. This second stile is marked by a stout wooden post which supports a strand of barbed wire. Signs around here are non-existent.

Continue NE towards the copse of trees ahead which locate the sheep pens at Pasture Barn, passing a dew pond on your L in your final approach. At the compound, use the W-stile to the R of the gate ahead to cross the next boundary wall. A gravel track then leads off, veering R through a metal gate. Start along this track but before it sweeps R bear off L, heading towards the lower corner of the field. Walk NE and use an S-stile over a stone wall. Turn L along the surfaced lane on the far side and progress N. A short distance further on, ignore a path off to the R by continuing up the modest incline straight ahead towards Town Head, about 1 km (about ½ mile) further N. The lane passes through Back o'th' Hill Farm *en route*. When you reach High Stool Farm, follow the lane as it bends, first to the R and then L, and ignore public footpaths on both sides.

The lane merges with a wider road and the route continues northwards in the direction signed to 'Chelmorton 2¼' along part of the Limestone Way. The major road linking Chelmorton with Sheldon is then crossed; after this, a straightish diagonal leads marginally uphill. Turn R when you reach a T-junction, head towards the crest of the hill

7:4 *Looking across a dew pond down towards the A6(T) road and Priestcliffe*

but just over 150 paces further on turn L along another walled way to resume progress northwards. This part of the route is often churned up by tractors so in wet conditions you can expect more clogging mud along here. When you reach a trio of gates, veer L to pass through a G-stile adjacent to the gate furthest to the L. This is at a point where a footpath connects with the walled track via an S-stile on your L. Your continuation direction remains to the N. A short distance further on, the track bends sharply L before winding back down the steeper slope ahead. This is near Five Wells shown on the OLM. There are revealing views in fine weather from here, including one of your continuation route northwards beyond the A6(T) road down below. This continuation is towards Miller's Dale, across rolling countryside, liberally covered with trees and enclosed pastures. A curved rough track leads through a wooden gate down to the trunk road, which is reached at the Waterloo Inn (MR 132714).

7:5 *Vapour trails above the tumulus near Priestcliffe Hall*

The way to Tideswell *(Allow 2½ hours)*

Cross the busy A6(T) road and proceed along Priestcliffe Road, directly opposite. At the next crossroads, turn L along the road signed to 'Priestcliffe Ditch – Blackwell – Miller's Dale'. Keep straight on when the road bends to the L, to continue northwards along a wide gravel path which is another part of the Limestone Way. This leads down to Miller's Dale about 1 km (½ mile) ahead. The ground on your L drops towards the hamlet of Blackwell, whils grassy limestone slopes rise uniformly to your R. The going underfoot here is usually sound, even in the wettest of weather conditions. The shallow descent is over firm ground between limestone walls and shaded by willow trees, mixed further down with hawthorn and elderberry bushes. This stretch is particularly relaxing. Then more spectacular views begin to emerge over on your L across the greenery of Blackwell Dale towards the merged gorge of Chee Dale and Miller's Dale, each with their steep, tree-covered sides.

During the prolonged, gradual descent, disregard a track leading uphill to the R. As you round a bend to the R the scale of the Chee Dale/Miller's Dale chasm becomes more apparent, ahead and below to your L. There are massive exposed rock faces from former quarrying operations on the far slopes of the wide valley but these are dwarfed by the overall grandeur of the surrounding scenery. The way continues to wind downhill, now over an upgraded surface of compressed stones. The distinctive pointed hillock which appears across the valley straight ahead is Knot Low. The route descends to the B6049 road which connects Miller's Dale with the A6(T) road. Cross the road and then use it to walk downhill to reach and cross over the River Wye at MR 137732.

Turn L up the road signed to 'Wormhill', immediately after crossing over the river. At the first bend, branch off L to climb the steep gradient of a railed, stepped footpath, immediately after passing through a wooden gate. This path is waysigned to 'Monsal Trail', as is another path to the L along the riverside; this leads W to Chee Dale. On reaching the top of the flight of steps, turn R to continue E along the Monsal Trail, an excellent, wide pathway of compacted basalt. Pass the former railway station of Miller's Dale, which has toilets and, during the summer, a mobile information carvan. Immediately afterwards, cross high above the valley over the former railway viaduct by the one of two impressively high bridges that remain open for walkers. Peep over the side to see the River Wye directly below. On the far side of the bridge you will spot some lime kilns above to your R and these deserve at least a cursory inspection.

Having returned to the trail, continue to walk E down the wide valley of Miller's Dale, passing through two shallow, tree-fringed cuttings. After walking along the Monsal Trail for about 1½ km

(1 mile) you will reach the point where a path signed to 'Ravenstor' leads down the steep, wooded slopes to your L. Follow this stepped way into the valley below: spectacular views of the River Wye and limestone cliff faces on the far side of the dale can be glimpsed through the foliage. A sturdy wood-and-concrete footbridge provides a secure crossing of the River Wye at one of its widest points. Turn R on the far bank, to continue downstream along a narrow lane, past the entrance to Ravenstor YH. On your L, spectacular cliffs of mixed limestone and igneous rock block off more distant views, but on your R there is more open scenery of high, tree-covered slopes lining the far side of the valley across the river.

Bear L when you reach the National Trust's Ravenstor car park at the entrance to Tideswell Dale. However, do not pass between the two boulders. Also avoid the rather obscure narrow path further L which leads beneath trees and then up the craggy cliff face to the YH. Instead, walk straight ahead, with the boulders to your L, to connect with the main path through Tideswell Dale. Turn L along this and continue NW up the dale. Tideswell is now little over 2 km (1¼ miles) away to the N. The ever-twisting dale is narrower and less deep than the wide chasm of Miller's Dale but it is also much more sheltered, with an abundance of flora and wildlife and several spectacular limestone buttresses and exposed rock faces. A good path of compacted earth, which is invariably well-drained, provides sure footing and allows you to concentrate on the scenery. The way up the dale, where

7:6 *Morning sunshine highlighting the rock faces lining Tideswell Dale*

height is gained very gradually, crosses a small stream by a wooden footbridge and beyond this, the dale widens out appreciably. Further on, when the paths divide, stick to the L-hand side of the stream, spurning another footbridge across the water. The stream is eventually crossed again higher up the valley as the two separate paths converge and you turn L here.

A short distance further on, after passing rock faces stained by leached mineral deposits, the way leads to the Tideswell Dale Information Area. This contains toilets, picnic facilities and a car park. To reach these facilities, always keep to the main valley path ignoring a side path leading back uphill on your R. A continuation path leads beneath mature beech trees towards Tideswell from the far end of the car park but ends all too soon at the road! However, you can escape for the time being along a grassy way which runs parallel to the road for some distance ahead. This path is accessed over a stile on your R. Along here, always keep to the lower, faintly defined path nearest to the road on your L. When you reach a barbed-wire fence blocking further progress along the grassy way, turn L over the W-stile, cross the road (B6049) and follow this the rest of the way into the village of Tideswell, now only a short distance to the N. The road leads uphill right into the centre of the village. Change sides as necessary to make use of the pavements. There are plenty of places in the village to satisfy your immediate needs, but Poppies Restaurant always looks inviting to me.

Alternatives

EXTENSIONS

Experienced climbers might consider one or more of the climbing routes up Aldery Cliff.

A less formidable extension near Aldery Cliff is to climb to the top of the hill of High Wheeldon when you reach MR 102662. The views along the vale of the Dove fully justify this short, sharp climb.

Chee Dale and Miller's Dale offer a variety of longer extensions. One suggestion is to walk W along Chee Dale for as long as you fancy before turning northwards to circle into Tideswell from the W, using the extensive network of connecting paths and back-roads. Another possibility is to continue E along Miller's Dale as far as Cressbrook before turning N up Cressbrook Dale to reach Tideswell via Litton.

EASIER ROUTES

The main route represents a very direct and interesting walk between Longnor and Tideswell. There are several alternative ways, but none of them offers any significant shortening of the overall route, which in any event is far from physically demanding.

Stage 8

TIDESWELL TO CASTLETON

8 The view northwards across Old Moor towards Mam Tor

Stage 8: TIDESWELL to CASTLETON

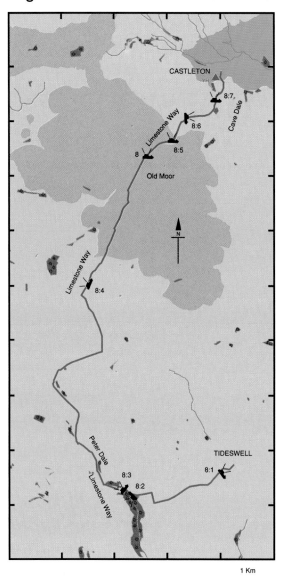

1 Km

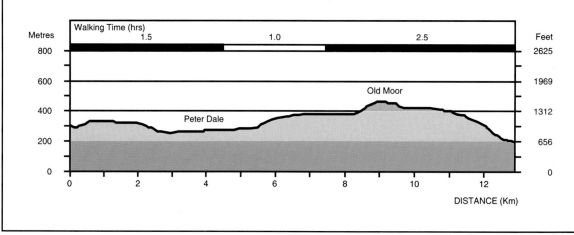

STARTING LOCATION

The village of Tideswell on the B6049 road.

The village lies just s of the main A623 road.

OLM 24/MR 151758. (Also use OLM 1.)

Car parking allowed in Market Square; spaces for about 15 to 20 cars.

Directions start from Market Square.

PUBLIC TRANSPORT

Principal town with extensive bus services.

These include connections with Bakewell, Baslow, Bradwell, Buxton, Calver, Castleton, Chapel-en-le-Frith, Chatsworth Park, Chesterfield, Derwent, Eyam, Glossop, Great Hucklow, Hartington, Hope, Litton, Manchester, Matlock, Monsal Head, Miller's Dale, Sheffield, Stockport, Stoney Middleton and Wardlow; and other places.

OVERVIEW/INTEREST

Another walk of outstanding variety.

Attractions of Tideswell, including the Cathedral of the Peak.

Spectacular limestone scenery of Peter Dale, Hay Dale and Cave Dale.

Makes use of significant sections of Limestone Way.

Crossing of high moorland terrain with wide open spaces.

Ever-changing views.

FOOTPATHS/WAYSIGNS

Oscillate from acceptable to very good.

Watch out for carelessly positioned barbed wire at certain stiles!

Route finding is relatively straightforward and very few uncertainties should arise.

Ground is mainly well drained and there are few seriously waterlogged areas.

Final descent into Castleton along a steep, rough path, in places across exposed bedrock.

OVERALL TIME ALLOWANCE 5 hours

Statistics		
Distance walked	**Km**	**Miles**
	12.9	8
Height climbed	**M**	**Feet**
	250	820
Principal heights	**M**	**Feet**
Old Moor	460	1510

The way to Dale Head *(Allow 1½ hours)*

During your stay at Tideswell you might consider visiting the fine church of Saint John the Baptist, otherwise known as the Cathedral of the Peak. The building urgently needs renovation and a restoration appeal has been launched, to which many walkers have already generously contributed. There is a magnificent flower festival in the church every year in early summer.

From the Market Square make your way, round by the church, back to the main road through the village and turn R along it, to walk s in the direction of Miller's Dale. Turn R into Parke Road, opposite the NatWest Bank, and walk W uphill passing the United Reformed Church. Turn L at the T-junction ahead and then immediately R, before bearing L along a bridleway to continue SW further uphill. The route leads into open countryside and there are good views to your rear over the housetops of Tideswell nestling among the hillsides. At the top of the brow use an S-stile on your R, between two gates, to enter a maze of dry-stone walling. This divides the rolling hills ahead into neat, enclosed pastures. The route continues W beside the first of these walls and you must maintain this direction through a G-stile which provides an entrance to the next field. Several more of these stiles follow in quick succession through a series of parallel dry-stone walls across your path. The route eventually bears L along a better defined diagonal.

More S- and G-stiles follow: watch out at one of these for some barbed wire close to the way across. Continue walking westwards, after some distance, downhill along a faintly defined path. Along here, locate a strategic stile through a wooden fence towards the far end of a field, where once more barbed wire is far too close for comfort! Beyond this, continue beside a stone wall on your L. Then bear slightly R away from the wall to cross another stile. The more complicated part of this initial section of the route ends when you reach a walled bridleway at MR 138751. Here there is a sign, No.217, belonging to the Peak and Northern Footpaths Society. Turn R along the bridleway (part of the Limestone Way) to walk N towards the road, with Monksdale House now in sight ahead. This connection can be somewhat muddy after heavy rain. Turn L at the junction near the house and walk downhill along the narrow, surfaced lane. This leads to the confluence of Monk's Dale to the SE and Peter Dale to the NW.

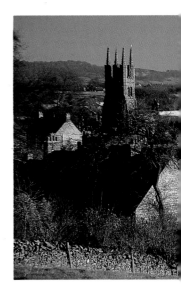

Above: 8:1 *Looking back over the roof-tops of Tideswell*

Below: 8:2 *The rolling green slopes beyond Monk's Dale*

Turn R off the road through a wooden G-stile when you reach the bottom of the valley, to enter the Nature Reserve (English Nature) extending WNW along Peter Dale. The Limestone Way also continues through this reserve. This entrance is a broad, flat, grassy expanse but it narrows quite rapidly and within a short distance you are walking through an enclosed dale hemmed in by steep, wooded limestone cliffs. Further into the dale, some of the side slopes expose their angled bedding planes as the grassy path surrenders to a rougher, stony way. The dry dale twists and turns, in a predominantly NW direction; just keep walking along the bottom of the dale and scrutinize any rock faces which catch your interest. From the enclosed rocky funnel, the route progresses into more open grassland again as the dale meanders northwards in a series of wide bends. Beyond a gateway through another dry-stone wall, the characteristics of the dale change back again to more vertical limestone cliffs which line the R-hand side of the valley ahead. These sheer rock-faces make compelling viewing as you pass beneath them along the grassy floor of a gorge-like section of the dale.

The flatter parts of Peter Dale are grazed by cattle and these animals often churn up the soft, lower ground. Do not be surprised if you come across muddy areas from time to time, particularly after prolonged wet weather. Otherwise, the going along the narrow dale is fine, and there is much to interest those with a keen eye.

Below: 8:3 *Limestone cliffs in Peter Dale*

The dale then reverts once again to a wider valley flanked by more gentle, rounded slopes and it is in these surroundings that the route reaches the dwellings of Dale Head at MR 123765. Here, a narrow lane crossing the Limestone Way is accessed by a W-stile. Turn R along the lane but within 50 paces turn off L to commence the next part of the route along the way signed to 'Peak Forest'.

The way to the A623 at Mount Pleasant Farm
(Allow 1 hour)

The narrow lane at Dale Head is vacated through a wooden S-stile. Then veer immediately L to walk between converging dry-stone walls, heading N along a grassy way. The first part of this section does become severely waterlogged after heavy rain and you may need to make a detour: try near the wall immediately on your R. There is much firmer ground ahead. After you have crossed a dry-stone wall by an S-stile, the dale bends progressively to your L towards NW where the valley system continues as Hay Dale. This is a somewhat shallower basin. The going here is along a firm, grassy channel and for some distance a dry-stone wall to your L indicates the correct way. The next feature is the bricked-up entrance to an abandoned mine shaft, with discarded equipment rusting away outside.

Further along the dale, an attractive line of trees to your L marks the continuation route through more limestone outcrops as the sides of the dale steepen once again. The trees develop into a shady avenue. The cooling foliage ceases when you come to a stone wall, crossed by a wooden S-stile to the L of a metal gate. This is at MR 118773. Bear R at the division of the ways ahead, to keep with the Limestone Way as it tracks NE along a walled track towards a rounded hillock directly ahead. This stretch is often heavy going over tractor-rutted ground. The way continues to climb, bending to the R in the process; on the way up, ignore a path leading off to the L. You then pass the place where 'Sheep Wash' is named on the OLM, though I have never come across it. As the track snakes towards the top of the brow, turn round to observe the extensive views of undulating countryside to your rear. These views confirm that the narrow, enclosed dales have now given way to open moorland.

A relatively straight stretch follows before the route leads to a back-lane at a T-junction. The approach is often muddy in winter. Turn L along the surfaced lane (which is still part of the Limestone Way) to progress further N, having rejected the public footpath off to your L just before joining the lane. The walk down the lane passes the entrance to Limestone Way Farm and then leads uneventfully to the main A623 road, opposite Mount Pleasant Farm. This farm is located at MR 125788.

The way to Castleton *(Allow 2½ hours)*

Cross the busy A623 road with care and turn L along it in the direction signed to 'Peak Forest ½ – Sparrowpit 2½'. Keep on the narrow grass verge where possible. After just over 100 paces, turn down the gated track on your R, which when last visited (winter 1994/95) was not signed, although it is still part of the Limestone Way. In good weather there are clear views from here, down to the L, of the village of Peak Forest to the W. A walled way then leads NNE, zigzagging up the grassy hillside and passing the knoll to your R, named 'Brood Low' on the OLM. The route passes through a gateway and over the brow of the slope ahead. When you reach a macadam lane, use the wooden S-stile on your L to gain access to it. Then bear R along the upgraded track to continue NE, passing beneath an electricity line and a telephone wire serving West View bungalow, on your R.

8:4 *Looking down on Peak Forest*

Further up the hill you reach the more substantial buildings of Copp Farm, from which footpaths radiate in several directions. The correct continuation route is straight ahead along the way signed to 'Castleton'. It leads further uphill, passing to the R of the farm buildings, and is accessed over a wooden S-stile, the sign at which is sometimes prostrate! Beyond this, veer L beside the perimeter wall of the adjacent field, walk past a metal gate to your L and then use the S-stile in a stone wall to the L of a narrow wooden gate to enter a definitive walled track leading further uphill. Your continuation route is still signed to 'Castleton' at this point and is to the NNE. The next, quite delightful section is by means of a firm, grassy path sheltered by limestone walling. Behind you there are views of a landscape stretching for kilometres in all directions between S and W.

Further up, past a W-stile and swing gate, in favourable weather conditions, there are compelling views ranging from the outline of Mam Tor and the undulating ridge leading E from it, terminating in Lose Hill, to the plateau of Kinder Scout stretching across your line of vision as a straight-edge ruler several kilometres long and at 600 m (2000 ft) effectively blocking off any more distant features to the N. Further W, the shape of South Head can be made out in very clear weather and to the R of this landmark the long, high profile of Rushup Edge looms, with the outlet of the air shaft from the railway tunnel visible between them to the NW.

8:5 *The descent towards Old Moor with Mam Tor in the distance*

STAGE 8   TIDESWELL TO CASTLETON

The continuation way leads gradually downhill round the hillside, following the winding course of a dry-stone wall to your L. Round the next bend, in clear weather, the conical shape of Win Hill appears far off to the NE; further away still, the Derwent Edges rise to the L of this weathered tor. An iron gate is then reached, near a dew pond. The way descends more steeply from here, still winding NE but into a gentler landscape of rounded, grassy slopes. A wire fence barring your way down is crossed at a P-stile and here your established NE diagonal way, by now a grassy track, keeps company for some distance with a stone wall on the L. This leads to a rather complicated intersection of paths and bridleways ahead.

These complications are dealt with by first passing through a G-stile to the L of a metal gate, walking straight on to climb over a W-stile next to a wooden gate (having crossed a wide track in between) and then passing through a relatively wide gap between a dry-stone wall and a wooden gate. Beyond these, bear marginally R to cross the next field on a straight diagonal, heading NE and towards the tip of Win Hill if in view. Another watering-hole is passed to your L. From here, the route undulates over grassy slopes along a clear, wide path towards which limestone walls converge. When you reach the division in the way ahead, fork R to pass through a metal swing gate as the path leads to the narrow, craggy gorge of Cave Dale. The upper reaches of this dale are attained after passing through a metal swing gate in a

8:6 *The approach to Cave Dale above Castleton*

dry-stone wall marking the boundary of Open Access Land. From here, the way bends round to the L to penetrate the narrowing and steepening dale.

The route then descends, first gradually along an obvious grassy path which further on is joined by a wide track coming in from the R. This track immediately branches off to the L as your descent continues ahead, increasingly more steeply through rugged terrain as the surface underfoot changes to a mixture of firm rock and loose stones. Be mindful where you are placing your feet on the rough, twisting and steep path, as the protruding limestone faces are quite slippery, particularly when wet. For a while the stony path becomes easier and grassy as the way leads between disused gateposts. Continue down-hill, crossing the remains of a shattered limestone wall to your R, after which the way leads through a swing gate. The gradient then steepens appreciably and the next section is along another section of narrow, stony pathway where appropriate care is again necessary.

Further into the descent, the ruins of Peveril Castle appear ahead to your L. These occupy a commanding position on a rocky limestone outcrop which lines the W flank of the now extremely steep-sided

8:7 Peveril Castle rising above the shadows of Cave Dale

dale. The rock-face on which the battlements have been constructed are almost sheer, providing the former occupants of the castle with a nigh impregnable fortress. The castle is now in the protective custody of English Heritage and their colourful brochure states: 'It is easy to see why William Peveril, one of William the Conqueror's most trusted knights, chose this site for his fortifications. For its dramatic situation on a triangular spur high above the town, Peveril commanded any approach from west, east and south. The north side was guarded by a high stone wall.'

In rainy weather, the rough path down past the castle ruins doubles as a watercourse and requires careful treading. Stop from time to time during your descent to absorb at your leisure the pearly white limestone columns and buttresses that line the dale, separated by sweeping slopes of bright, pea-green grasses. The overall effect is sensational.

A final narrow chink in the surrounding precipitous rock structures permits an exit via a gateway into the attractive village of Castleton, immediately below. Turn L along Pindale Road to pass (perhaps with some reluctance and induced delay), the well-patronized Hilary Beth's Tea Room, bearing first L and then R round the War Memorial triangle to pass by or into the YH. If the YH is not your final destination for the day, walk down Castle Street into the centre of the village.

Alternatives

EXTENSIONS
There is much to see and do in and around Castleton, including visits to the ruins of Peveril Castle and nearby Peak Cavern. Bear these sightseeing possibilities in mind when planning extensions of the walking route.

After crossing the main A623 road just to the SE of Peak Forest there is a maze of alternative longer and more circuitous routes into Castleton, to both W and E of the main route. The attractions to the W are Perry Dale and Eldon Hill, whilst to the E the vastness of Bradwell Moor and the paths crossing these uplands provide numerous possibilities for personally selected extension that can easily be planned by consulting the OLM.

EASIER ROUTES
It is possible to miss out Peter Dale and Hay Dale or the final adventurous descent along Cave Dale. The former may be achieved by using the minor lanes and tracks via Wheston to rejoin the main route at MR 128778, whilst Cave Dale may be avoided by keeping L when you reach the fork at MR 139816 and following the more gradual descent into Castleton along the footpath to the W of Cave Dale. These alternatives miss out so much: only use them if you feel you must.

Stage 9

CASTLETON TO HAYFIELD

9 *Morning sunshine illuminates South Head*

Stage 9: CASTLETON to HAYFIELD

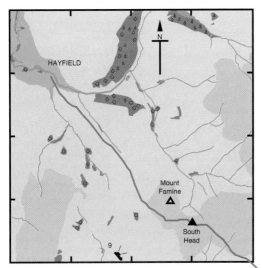

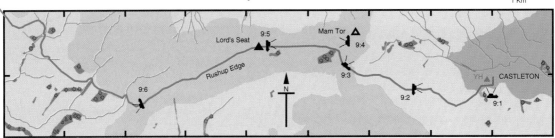

1 Km

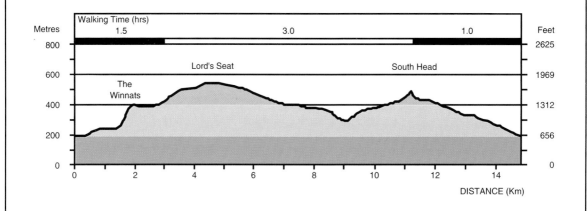

Map labels:

Inset map (top):
HAYFIELD
Mount Famine
South Head
9

Main map:
Lord's Seat — 9:5
Mam Tor — 9:4
9:3
9:2
9:1
Rushup Edge
9:6
YH CASTLETON
N

Elevation profile:

Walking Time (hrs)		
1.5	3.0	1.0

Metres — Feet

800 — 2625
600 — 1969
400 — 1312
200 — 656
0 — 0

The Winnats

Lord's Seat

South Head

DISTANCE (Km)
0   2   4   6   8   10   12   14

STARTING LOCATION

The village of Castleton on the A625 road.

The village lies towards the head of the Hope Valley, just below the Winnats Pass.

OLM 1/MR 150829.

Large car-parking area and toilets near centre of village.

Directions start from A625 through centre of village.

PUBLIC TRANSPORT

Extensive bus services linking Ashford, Bakewell, Bamford, Barnsley, Baslow, Bradwell, Buxton, Chatsworth, Chesterfield, Derwent, Edale, Glossop, Grindleford, Hartington, Hathersage, Hope, Huddersfield, Hyde, Ladybower, Manchester, Mansfield, Matlock, Monsal Head, Ripley, Rochdale, Sheffield, Tideswell, Winnats Pass and other places.

OVERVIEW/INTEREST

Great start through the Winnats Pass with its spectacular limestone cliffs.

Followed by welcome return to the shales and grits of the Dark Peak.

Elevated ridge walk along Rushup Edge.

Summit of South Head scaled.

Outstanding panoramic views for most of way, including those along Mam Tor Ridge.

Opportunities to visit Peak Cavern, Speedwell Cavern, Blue John Mines and Chestnut Centre.

FOOTPATHS/WAYSIGNS

Good and adequately signed for most of way.

Route mainly over firm, well-drained terrain.

The approach to and round South Head does become muddy after heavy rain (motor bikes churning up this section add to the problem).

Relatively few stiles and similar obstacles.

Only occasional rough ground to cross.

OVERALL TIME ALLOWANCE 5½ hours

Statistics		
Distance walked	**Km**	**Miles**
	14.8	9.2
Height climbed	**M**	**Feet**
	450	1475
Principal heights	**M**	**Feet**
Top of Winnats Pass	399	1310
Rushup Edge	540	1770
South Head	494	1620

The way to Mam Nick (*Allow 1½ hours*)

From the main A625 road through the village, turn up Castle Street by the Castle Hotel to walk southwards past the Parish Church of St Edmund, Castleton. The ruins of Peveril Castle are outlined at the top of the steep, grassy hillock directly ahead. (The views from these former battlements down across the Hope Valley are fantastic but English Heritage do not open the site until 10.00 a.m.) Turn R by the YH when you reach the T-junction ahead, to continue along the narrow lane signed to 'Peak Cavern' and then avoid the higher level ways leading directly to Peveril Castle. Peveril Outdoor and Travel Shop is passed immediately on your L as is a fish-and-chip shop. The outdoor shop does provide a most convenient place to acquire any urgently needed equipment or clothing.

Continue downhill with the profiles of the Winnats Pass and Mam Tor now looming straight ahead. Mam Tor is also known as the Shivering Mountain because its composition of alternating horizontal layers of softer shales and harder grits renders it unstable; it is in fact continually slipping into the valley and has completely demolished the road snaking up its slopes.

Across the stream of Peakshole Water, ignore the branch path on your L leading up to Peak Cavern (unless you wish to have a peep into this underground cavity). After overcoming the gradient of Goosehill, avoid the lane on your L as you continue SW to reach and follow a rocky pathway. This leads through a metal gate into open country. From here, a narrow path – a mixture of stones, compact earth and grass – bends round the hillside beside a stone wall towards the Winnats Pass, ahead to your R. Further height is gained along here and the most superb views are progressively revealed of the wide, tree-lined Hope Valley, including the nearby villages of Castleton and Hope. The southerly slopes of the Mam Tor to Lose Hill Ridge sweep down into the valley's flat basin with its several watercourses, including the Odin Sitch. In clear weather, look NNE and NE respectively to spot the pointed tors of Lose Hill and Win Hill.

9:1 *Castleton and Lose Hill from the ramparts of Peveril Castle*

9:2 *Looking east along the Hope Valley from the top of the Winnats Pass*

Beyond a G-stile, the opening of which is protected by a metal flap, the route connects with the narrow but well-used improvised road through Winnats Pass (Mam Tor having permanently blocked the former A625). Turn L along the upgraded road and walk uphill past the Speedwell Cavern. (A visit to the bottomless underground pit at the far end of this cave system involves an unusual boat journey: your captain for the day will cram you full of knowledge of the cavern's history and the reason for the partly water-filled tunnel that gives you access to this pit.) There is a well-stocked gift shop outside the cavern. To avoid traffic, walk through the car parking area opposite, exiting from this over the S-stile in the far wall, and follow the narrow path adjacent to a limestone wall to your R.

A rough, narrow way then climbs steeply westwards to the top of the craggy limestone spurs flanking the northern side of the Winnats Pass. In clear weather this ascent offers superb views: limestone pillars and stacks lining the gorge down on your L and also to your rear, and wide open spaces when looking E along the flatness of Hope Valley, with Castleton and Hope spreadeagled far below. However, be ever mindful of where you are treading for the worn limestone slabs which

form part of this climb can become extremely slippery, particularly when either water or ice is about. Part way up, ignore a way leading over a stile to your R. After this the still steep slopes become more grassy as most of the protruding limestone outcrops are left below. For some way along the uppermost slopes there is a wire fence to accompany your progress but be careful of the top strand, which is barbed. You can pause for breath at the top and take in the superb views below and the more distant panorama. The positions of most of the latter have previously been mentioned, apart from the landscapes further W where part of your continuation route along Rushup Edge is now revealed.

Head westwards from the high ground above the Winnats by initially passing over a wooden P-stile to your R. Walk for a short distance directly in line with Mam Tor and pass through a wooden gate to your L. Bear further L following this, round the contours of the slope to your L, maintaining a more or less constant height. This

Above: 9:3 *Back Tor and Lose Hill seen from the road near Blue John Cavern*

section is along a faintly discernible, wide, grassy path across open slopes. The way then tracks further L, to head due W. You come to a stile breaching a stone wall a short distance from Winnats Head Farm, away on the L. From here, continue across the next field to reach and cross a minor road (the B6061). This crossing is at MR 128830 and entry and exit are through wide G-stiles. Then select the R-hand fork in the path ahead to walk round the appropriately named 'Windy Knoll'. In following the wide grassy sward, keep tight hold of your hat!

The way then connects with the western approaches of the A625 road, undermined further E. Cross this on a diagonal to your L and head up the grassy slopes extending towards the top of Mam Tor, heading for the distinctive fault of Mam Nick, now visible on the horizon to the L of the higher ground of Mam Tor. Towards the top of the slope, a fence is reached; immediately across this, turn L to continue up a narrow, grassy path which then bisects the main path connecting the car park below with the summit of Mam Tor. The crossing of this is on an acute diagonal. Walk straight on, to reach and cross the minor road leading from the A625 into the Vale of Edale to the N.

The way to South Head *(Allow 3 hours)*

At Mam Nick, leave the minor road by climbing over an S-stile. After this, head NW up the grassy slopes leading towards Rushup Edge. This high-level spur leads further W for about 3.5 km (just over 2 miles) before terminating towards the course of the A625 road, which is reached again at MR 093825.

In the meantime there have been many new interesting views. At the crest of the ridge, for example, you can look down into the

Right: 9:4 *Soaring above Edale from a launching pad near Mam Tor*

picturesque valley of Edale with its neatly enclosed pastures. Protecting this sheltered valley, on the far side, is the great bulk of the southern slopes of Kinder Plateau. This land mass rises to 600 m (2000 ft) and its gritty edges, indented with numerous cloughs and fault-lines, are strewn with boulders and rocky outcrops of bewildering shapes and sizes (you will have the opportunity to inspect some of these closely during the final stage). To the E the undulating slopes of the ridge connecting Mam Tor with Lose Hill fade in the distance but you have already explored this ground from Hollins Cross eastwards during the first stage of this long-distance walk (p.34).

Continue along the ridge, taking the occasional stile in your stride and progressively gaining height. The way along the crest of the spur is obvious – a wide, somewhat eroded and well-trodden path. Keep always to the main path leading westwards which hugs the course of a dry-stone wall on the L. The apex of the ridge stands at 540 m (1770 ft) and there is a tumulus nearby at Lord's Seat. The positions of the extensive views to be observed in fine weather from this elevated viewing position have all been previously mentioned. The long, shallow descent back to the road is usually uneventful and the distant views quickly become blocked by the sides of a narrow gully.

9:5 *Looking eastwards along Rushup Edge towards Mam Tor and Lose Hill*

As you approach the road, there is a panorama of raking, bluish escarpments and hilly spurs receding one behind the other into the distant SW to your L. These hills encircle the village of Chapel-en-le-Frith. A final wooden S-stile has to be mounted before the A625 road is eventually reached again. During this final approach, the pointed shape of South Head puts in a first appearance in the distant NW. (You will be standing on the top of this before too long.) Hayfield, your final destination for the day, lies not far beyond and it is all downhill from South Head. During the shallow descent to the road, be careful to ignore a side path on the R leading off towards Edale via Barber Booth.

There is no need to proceed along the roadway; instead, bear R before you reach it and continue beside the stone wall and use the grassy strip of land directly ahead to reach the continuation track which then leads NW towards South Head. Many walkers now do so and this short, connecting passage appears, at least for the time-being, to be tolerated. If not, use the side of the road to access the public footpath ahead on the R.

By either approach, turn R to continue your descent, now along a well-established track. The route crosses a tiny watercourse at an acute bend to the L and from here you are on your way up again, albeit along a far from demanding gradient. Several stiles and gates are encountered before a copse of deciduous trees (Tom Moor Plantation) is passed, nearby to your L. More of these clusters follow, lining both sides of the track, as your route now winds downhill. Beyond a G-stile at a metal gate, the way drops much more steeply along a rough, stony path which often doubles as a significant watercourse! This is at Roych Clough where two streams have to be forded at the bottom and where another wooden gate temporarily bars your progress. Your route then winds equally steeply and almost as quickly back uphill. This section is favoured by high-speed motor-bike riders seeking to improve their scrambling techniques, so watch out!

The often churned-up ground bends round a derelict building on the L as your path winds uphill along rutted, grassy slopes beside a dry-stone wall. Further on, a straightish diagonal leads more gently uphill along another rough, stony section of the way. Passing through two more metal gates, the winding track crosses further grassy slopes, continuously gaining height. Again, the ground along here can become waterlogged with significant muddy patches appearing after heavy rain. The track continues to climb, very gradually, eventually reaching the col directly below the much steeper grassy slopes leading to the summit of South Head. An interesting feature by the side of the track before you reach the brow of the slope is a signed frog-breeding pond. (However, its surface is usually blanketed with a dense screen of water plants and algae, making it nigh impossible for you to observe the underwater antics.) After passing over a wooden S-stile at another

9:6 *Coming off Rushup Edge in gathering twilight*

metal gate, turn sharp L at the col and climb WNW to reach the top of South Head. This is only a short distance further on and higher up, but do mentally prepare yourself for one false horizon on your way to the summit. Once more, there are rewarding views in all directions from the top, including those to the NW towards the sister peak of Mount Famine and those to the NE towards the rim of Kinder Scout.

The way to Hayfield *(Allow 1 hours)*

Start your descent from South Head along the grassy path leading WNW to reconnect with the main track, leading round the hillside at a constant height, below. The first 50 paces or so from the top are steep, down a rough, slippery slope of tufted grass. At the bottom of the steeper section, bear L and follow the main track, immediately passing between two huge stone gateposts. In wet conditions, more boggy areas lie ahead, some of these filling quite deep rutted tracks. It is sometimes necessary to make a detour along the higher slopes to the R. After passing through yet another metal gate, an obvious walled track leads sedately downhill into the outskirts of the village of Hayfield at Highgate, less than 3 km (under 2 miles) to the NW. The ground underfoot now improves in direct ratio to height surrendered and the final part of the descent is along a macadam surface.

During the extended uneventful descent, be careful to avoid all paths leading off to either L or R. These include one particularly tempting opening on your R which will lead you back into open countryside, eastwards towards Edale and several other attractive locations. After passing the 30-mph traffic sign, and way past Highgate Farm, you will eventually reach Hayfield along Highgate Road. Continue into the centre of the village at St Matthew's Parish Church by way of Church Street, where there are several shops, cafés and nearby toilet facilities.

Alternatives

EXTENSIONS

There are many attractions convenient to Stages 8 and 9, such as caverns and castles, to absorb any free time that strong and fast walkers may have at their disposal. For this reason, the suggested extensions are confined to those which are of modest proportions only.

One other attraction is the Chestnut Centre near Slackhall. This houses a collection of owls and otters kept in a fairly natural environment, incorporating a bluebell dell. After you have descended from Rushup Edge to the A625 road, do not turn R along the track as described for the main route; instead continue WSW along the path leading across Breck Edge and cross the A625 road lower down the slope. The Chestnut Centre is on the far side, on your R, at MR 076819. Do not delay too long here, for the return to reach the main route again at MR 072838 by way of Malcoff Farm and Shireoaks to the N adds considerably to the detour.

Perhaps of more interest to strong walkers is the scaling of Mam Tor and/or Mount Famine. The short extension to the top of Mam Tor could be extended by walking eastwards along the ridge as far as Hollins Cross. Combined with Stage 1, this would give the added satisfaction of having walked the complete length of the ridge from Rushup Edge to Win Hill during this long-distance route. If you decide to tackle this, bear in mind that you will have to return to Mam Nick, regaining in this process all height surrendered in reaching Hollins Cross.

EASIER ROUTES

This Stage is fairly direct and there are no convenient options for significantly shortening the way. However, there are two possibilities for making the main route less challenging.

The first of these is near the start: instead of scaling the rough, rocky ground to the top of the Winnats, simply use the wide grass verges bordering the roadside to walk through the pass. The scenery remains fantastic. When you reach the top of the road, continue along it, then turn R and return to the main route by passing through the wide G-stile at MR 128830. The second short-cut is even more straightforward: do not go to the top of South Head but simply keep to the path which leads round this peak at a constant elevation until you reach MR 058846.

Stage 10

HAYFIELD TO EDALE

*10 Above Kinder Reservoir on the wide, open slopes
leading to Sandy Heys*

Stage 10: HAYFIELD to EDALE

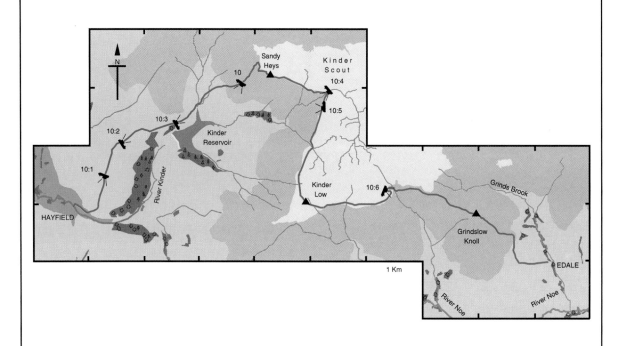

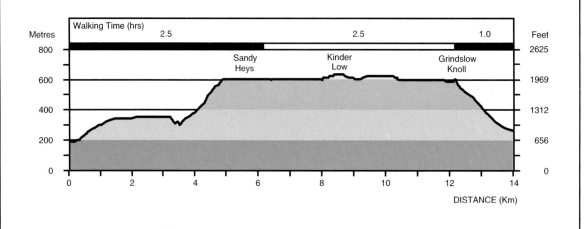

STARTING LOCATION

Village of Hayfield on the A624 road, between Glossop and Chapel-en-le-Frith.

OLM 1/MR 037868.

Large, well-appointed car-parking area just off A6015 road, to W of village centre. Also information centre, picnic area and toilets.

Directions start from centre of village at Parish Church.

PUBLIC TRANSPORT

Bus routes 355 (Hayfield, New Mills, Stepping Hill Hospital), 358 (Hayfield, New Mills, Marple, Stockport), 361 (Glossop, New Mills, Stockport), 403 (Crystal Peaks, Chesterfield, Edale, Hayfield), 901 (Huddersfield, Glossop, Hartington, Crich) and 902 (Huddersfield, Glossop, Buxton, Macclesfield).

OVERVIEW/INTEREST

Grand finale to this long-distance walk.

Picturesque start, gradually gaining height, up to Kinder Reservoir.

Followed by steep climb up to Sandy Heys on Kinder Edge.

A taste of Kinder Scout; crossing of the Downfall and section along south-western edges of plateau.

Fantastic rock formations and scattered boulders including Noe Stool, Pym Chair, Wool Packs and Crowden Tower.

Route climbs to summit of Grindslow Knoll.

Pleasant descent into Edale.

Superb, panoramic views all day long, given fine weather.

FOOTPATHS/WAYSIGNS

Considering the rough terrain, footpaths vary from adequate to good.

Not an abundance of signs but very few of these needed.

Sections of route are across streams, boulders and rocky outcrops.

Some peaty, boggy ground has to be covered but this hardly approaches 'peat hag' demands!

Perfect acclimatization for tackling the more challenging high, acid moorlands of Bleaklow and Black Hill on future occasions.

OVERALL TIME ALLOWANCE   6 hours

Statistics		
Distance walked	**Km**	**Miles**
	14.1	8.8
Height climbed	**Metres**	**Feet**
	560	1835
Principal heights	**M**	**Feet**
Kinder Low	633	2075
Crowden Tower	619	2030
Grindslow Knoll	601	1970

The way to Kinder Downfall (Allow 2½ hours)

From the Parish Church of St Matthew in the centre of Hayfield Village, cross the River Sett/Kinder by the footbridge alongside the road and turn R up Bank Street. This leads to Kinder Road; veer R here and walk gently uphill SE, away from the village. The road bends sharply to the L and then less severely R. Beyond these curves and just past Holly Farm, be careful not to miss a turning on the L with a not too obvious entrance, up a flight of steps, to a very important and well-used footpath. A sign here reads 'Snake Inn footpath via William

Clough and the Ashop Valley (Dedicated for ever – May 29 1897)'. The initial section of this footpath winds uphill on a stone-and-gravel surface and along here the first of several distinctive iron K-gates is reached. During this part of the gradual ascent, there are revealing views behind you over the village of Hayfield in the valley below, surrounding its towered church. The rounded, craggy hillsides beyond form a wide ridge rising to Chinley Churn to the SW and Lantern Pike to the NW.

Continue gaining height along the obvious wide path which leads in a predominantly easterly direction. Further up, you will be able to spot again the pointed outlines of Mount Famine and South Head, now a considerable distance away to the SE. Then keep L in order to avoid walking along a farm cart-track leading off more to the R. The second iron K-gate is reached, this one providing passageway through a dry-stone wall just above a tiny copse of beech trees, through which there are dramatic views down to Hayfield. The next K-gate is just beyond these trees and marks a change in the composition of the path, which narrows along a surface of compacted sand and sections of peat. After the route has curved to the R and you have passed through another K-gate, in clear weather you will see a superb mountainous landscape rising ahead. This vista of vast moorland is seen to perfection in late August/early September when the ranging slopes are covered with heather in full bloom. The views include Leygatehead Moor and its high point, The Knott. From this observation point, the direction to continue in is NE.

A short distance further on, the first clear sightings of Kinder Scout should appear. These slopes dominate the far distance, away to the ENE and ahead to your R. Even from this distance, the sheer size and flatness of the massive high-level plateau present a compelling attraction. This unforgettable scene is at its best just after daybreak on a clear, frosty morning with a dusting of snow.

Nearer, in the middle distance, a white-painted shooting cabin comes into view and this unpretentious building blends surprisingly well with its surroundings. The fifth and final iron K-gate marks the boundary of open country and signals the point of entry to the National Trust High Peak Estate. It also signifies that 'going up' is over for some distance ahead! A wide, sandy path leads off from here, bisecting at a fairly constant height the heather-covered moorland. Then a path up from Glossop merges from the L. Following this, the continuation route bends to the R to cross, almost immediately, a patch of deep bog – fortunately by means of wooden bridging. Along here, your path is signed 'To the Snake Inn and to Edale'.

During the next section of your elevated route, several less interesting ways up from Hayfield (in the form of paths and bridleways) merge from the R. The next sight of significant interest is the irregular shape of Kinder Reservoir. These catchment waters fill several cloughs which contain feeder streams running into the indented reservoir. A narrow path of compacted earth leads further E, high above the reservoir, as you head more directly towards Kinder Scout. There is more

10:2 *The grouse moors to the west of Kinder Scout*

10:3 *The narrow path snaking east towards Kinder Scout above Kinder Reservoir*

superb scenery along here, particularly on sunny days when even the tiniest white cloud is faithfully mirrored on the surface of the waters below. The way descends marginally and then undulates as the reservoir is passed.

Just before reaching the southern entrance to William Clough, the rougher part of the stage commences. The start to this is down a steep side route which is accessed by turning R and using the narrow path to descend gingerly to a crossing point near where the stream flowing down William Clough enters Kinder Reservoir. The crossing, by means of a bridge, is at MR 060887 and the approach to it is to the NE.

At the bottom of the slope, ignore the path leading off on your L into the confines of William Clough. Instead, cross the peaty stream by the wooden footbridge, then engage low gear and bear L up the steep, stepped path ahead. The surface quickly changes to a narrow, diagonal path (not marked on the OLM) and further height is gained to the NE over the brow of the slopes to the W of Hollin Head. Above this immediate horizon the rim of Kinder Plateau, your next major objective, fills the skyline directly ahead. Your continuation way for some distance can now be made out as a faint ribbon winding up the vast, grassy slopes ahead to the R. The way continues to climb, now to the ENE, towards the more craggy spur above.

Following the crossing of a small, reeded stream, the gradient steepens appreciably and from here a better-defined path, the surface of which alternates between compacted soil and grass, leads higher up the slopes, invariably tracking ENE. The path leads to the base of even steeper slopes and then traverses up those to your R along an indistinct, stony, diagonal path which in places will challenge your navigational skills to the full.

Continue to head NE up the rough slopes of tufted grasses which, when you come off the faint path, are hard on the ankles. A short distance further up, be particularly careful to locate and follow the indistinct path as it bears full-R to gain the crest of the spur and then follow this higher up the mountain. After you have made this connection, the going becomes physically less demanding and much easier to track correctly. There is even time to turn around to admire the fine, open views across Kinder Reservoir, now left far below you. The route bears slightly left to follow the pointed spur, up craggy slopes towards the westerly rim of Kinder, just above. Near the top, turn R along the wide, sandy edge path and thread your way to the nearby high-point of Sandy Heys. This is reached at MR 072893.

More boulders, slabs and rocky outcrops, many weathered into extraordinary shapes, are passed in quick succession as the obvious path leads along the irregular edge. The stacked boulders range from tiny fragments to gigantic masses of broken-off chunks of rock. You are now treading along part of the famous Pennine Way footpath and will continue to do so for some distance. With much to explore, the walk of just over 1 km (about ¾ mile) along the edge to reach Kinder Downfall soon passes. A solitary wooden stile has to be crossed; immediately over this minor obstacle be careful to select the higher path to the L. The Downfall is a jumble of shattered rocks which literally 'fall down' almost vertically into the deep void below. This natural fault is at its most spectacular in frosty conditions when the stream is

10:4 *A snow-covered Kinder Downfall*

in flood and there is a wind blowing against the current of the water. Then the combination of huge, dangling icicles and freezing spray being blown back over the rocks produces perfect winter scenery. The relative shelter afforded by the boulders lining the Downfall renders this the ideal lunch spot.

The way to Grindslow Knoll *(Allow 2½ hours)*

After crossing the Downfall, bear R along the continuation of Kinder Edge and walk ssw for some distance across a mixture of fixed rock slabs and more precariously balanced boulders. The way initially follows the fault-line of the Downfall but it then bears L and more southerly to cross another small clough by its rocky bed. It keeps to the edge, tracking ssw along a clear path; further on, intermittent cairns confirm the direction. There is more than one way along the edge and these alternatives (not all recognized routes) run parallel to each other within a relative narrow height band. Their surfaces vary considerably and I suggest that you follow a path with the best surface until you become dissatisfied with it and then search for another parallel one, making sure that you do not surrender any appreciable height and that you continue to maintain progress towards ssw. The surfaces include dry rock, loose stones, shale, sand, peat and bog – a typical gritstone cocktail!

10:5 *Looking west, back towards Hayfield, from Kinder Edge*

Your next certain objective is the trig point at Kinder Low, MR 079871. This concrete mound stands at 633 m (2075 ft) and is the highest point of the entire route. It lies to the L of the rim of the plateau and just above the serrated, boulder-strewn edge. To get there you will need to cross an exposed strip of peat and sand, the shallow humps of which may be firm in dry conditions but become like a continuous peat hag in wet seasons. You can glean an inkling of the oozy vastness of Kinder Plateau when you stare westwards into the inhospitable terrain of peat hags: these occupy some of the most difficult ground anywhere across Kinder Scout and they should only be entered by those well prepared for the challenges which lie in wait. Instead, your own passage is to follow a ESE bearing from the trig point, departing along an initially sandy pathway that threads between mounds of peat. Ahead to the SE are the first glimpses into the Vale of Edale flanked by the undulating ridge of Mam Tor and Lose Hill.

The clear way soon dissipates into an uncharted peaty landscape but the mixture of heather, bilberry and grasses do provide relatively firm going. Keep to your established bearing across this terrain, forging your own crossing where the way is too indistinct to follow. (I have crossed this way on numerous occasions and I cannot recall using exactly the same course twice!) You soon reach another distinct path along the edge, this one twisting predominantly W to E. Bearing L and to the E along this path, you immediately reach more rock formations, including Noe Stool after passing a massive cairn. Rock slabs and boulders abound along the next section eastwards. The going can become tiresome in heavy, wet conditions and you should keep to the clearly defined footpath along the edge. This ranges in quality from clinging bog to good, dry, sand and sometimes traverses rock slabs. Then the Wool Packs are entered – a vast area of scattered boulders of all shapes and sizes, some apparently welded together in groups whilst others are huge, isolated rocks reminiscent of erratic boulders from an ice age.

The fascinating route continues eastwards past the relatively safe, rounded outcrop of rocks forming Crowden Tower, set against a striking backcloth. The next feature of note is the crossing of Crowden Clough. The small stream is forded by means of horizontal bedding slabs, just to the NE of the Tower. The actual crossing of the water is easy enough but exercise care on the steepish, quite badly eroded and narrow descent in this clough!

After the crossing, continue eastwards as before, along an improved section of path which has a well-drained, sandy surface. About 1 km (over ½ mile) beyond Crowden Clough, fork R and walk ESE directly towards Grindslow Knoll, the prominent peak on the skyline directly ahead. A wide, obvious path snakes up over ground which is liable to become boggy at almost any time of the year to the drier, steeper final approach slopes which lead to the top of the

10:6 *The rocks of Crowden Tower provide fine views eastwards towards Grindslow Knoll*

mountain. This is the last climb of the day and of the entire walk, so make the most of it!

The summit of Grindslow Knoll provides a fine viewing platform in clear weather. Most of the features to be observed from here have already been described but in addition there are particularly revealing views down into the long reaches of Grindsbrook Clough tearing into the underbelly of Kinder from the lower ground around Edale. This vantage point reveals most of the secrets of the Vale of Edale and also most of the remainder of your journey around the Peak.

The way back to Edale *(Allow 1 hour)*

Make your final descent to the SE. The initial section is quite steep along a stone and sandy path through a craggy area of exposed rock. The path points more or less directly towards the village of Edale, your journey's end, though this does not come into view for some distance yet. During the descent you can identify the eroded, wide path on the far side of Grindsbrook that zigzags up to the rocks of Ringing Roger further E along Kinder Edge. Your own path bends with the contours of the falling slope and keeping to it presents little challenge. Round a bend in the hillside, the buildings of Edale come into sight below to the L, in the SE. A church with a spire is the focal point of the cluster of dwellings.

The very obvious path descends down a long, straight traverse and the crossing of a stile below marks the boundary of your departure from open country into inhabited lands once more. A pleasant grassy path completes the hilly bit. When you reach the flat land below, do take care to follow the signed 'Pennine Way' footpath in the correct direction, for a R turn might take you on another lap of this long-distance walk, in the reverse direction! A final short walk to the E will bring you back to the top end of Edale at the point where it all started, at the Nag's Head Inn.

Alternatives

EXTENSIONS

There will be tiger-walkers amongst the pack who will relish finishing this long-distance walk with a significantly more challenging trek than that suggested for the main route. If this applies to you, read on!

When you reach the northern tip of Kinder Reservoir, instead of descending to the R along the steep, narrow path, continue climbing NNE up William Clough to reach and cross the Pennine Way at MR 063902. Then continue along the Snake Path route, descending eastwards along Ashop Clough into the Woodlands Valley. Use Gate Side Clough to climb on to Kinder Edge, reaching this at the rocky outcrop of Seal Stones (MR 114888). Walk round the edge path above Blackden Moor until the path begins to veer E again, at MR 117883, and then branch off to the R to cross Kinder Plateau. There follows a relatively straightforward southern crossing of the formidable peat hags covering most of Kinder Scout at one of its narrowest and least formidable points. Some deviations from a direct line will almost certainly be necessary but unerringly head towards the higher ground of Hartshorn ahead. This is passed to your R just before reaching the southern edge of the plateau. There, turn R and westwards along the edge path and descend into Edale by way of Grindsbrook Clough.

EASIER ROUTES

There will be other walkers who, towards the end of this challenging long-distance walk, will prefer to have a final stage which is appreciably less demanding than the main route described. The terrain between Hayfield and Edale accommodates such a variant with ease.

Walk past the entrance to the Snake Inn footpath on the outskirts of Hayfield by continuing eastwards along the lane to reach Bowden Bridge. Cross the River Kinder here and use the lanes and tracks leading up to and then around Tunstead Clough Farm, to access the footpaths leading SE across Harry Moor to link up at MR 073862 with the wide, walled bridleway coming up Oaken Clough. Follow this further eastwards past Edale Cross to reach Jacob's Ladder. Descend along the refurbished zigzag path into the Vale of Edale below. Then walk along the valley until you reach Upper Booth, where you turn L to use part of the Pennine Way flagged footpath to lead you back to the top of the village of Edale, joining up with the main route shortly before you reach the Nag's Head Inn.

ACCOMMODATION AND TRANSPORT

ACCOMMODATION

Finding suitable accommodation quickly and simply is an important ingredient in the planning of this walk. The design of the long-distance route ensures that those who undertake the entire walk over consecutive days can find somewhere convenient to stay overnight in each of the selected villages along the way. An accommodation register is provided in Table 8 (pp. 162–171) for each of the overnight stops, covering as wide a price range as possible – youth hostels, picturesque farms, comfortable guest houses and well-appointed, medium-sized hotels of up to three-star status.

Considerable care has been exercised in compiling the register, which is based on three reliable sources: *The Rambler's Yearbook and Accommodation Guide 1995*, *The Peak National Park Accommodation and Catering Guide 1995* and personal contacts by the author. The information in the register was up to date at the time of writing but it would be wise to check the latest rates and facilities when making your booking. All these establishments have been contacted directly and it is believed that all of them will extend a warm welcome to walkers.

Some of the villages can offer more extensive accommodation than others, but even the locations with the most limited facilities are situated relatively close to other villages or larger towns. If problems are experienced at a particular place, the walking party will be able to use public transport or local taxi services (see p.160) to take them to a larger conurbation with more extensive facilities. On the following morning the party can return by similar means to the same point on the walking route. The towns of Buxton, Bakewell, Matlock and Ashbourne are particularly suitable for such use.

In planning your walk, it is tempting to try to arrange overnight accommodation at all 10 consecutive locations, on a night-by-night basis, well in advance of your intended departure date. This seems to be particularly appealing if you are walking during a popular time of the year, such as the school holidays or over bank holiday weekends. There are some drawbacks to such plans. Firstly, some establishments will not accept one-night bookings during popular holiday periods well in advance, though they are more than happy to reserve these a

Tissington Spires, Dove Dale

day or two beforehand if space is available. The other weakness is that flexibility is seriously constrained: one day's unexpected misfortune could jeopardize all your careful forward planning!

In the majority of situations it is better to fix your accommodation in advance for the first night and perhaps the next one or two, and then roll these arrangements forward on a day-by-day basis. If you find a place very much to your liking, ask its proprietors to recommend similar accommodation at the next location.

Youth hostels

The Peak District is well served by youth hostels. Those at or near Edale, Hathersage, Bakewell, Youlgreave, Ilam, Hartington, Buxton and Castleton are either on or within convenient transportation distance of the walking route. The addresses, opening periods, facilities available and other useful information about these hotels are obtainable from the latest edition of the *YHA Accommodation Guide*, which is issued free of charge to members.

TRANSPORT

Buses and trains

The Peak District is within easy reach of three densely populated regions: Greater Manchester and Merseyside lying to the west of the National Park; Sheffield and the West Riding of Yorkshire to the east;

and the industrial Midlands to the south. Mainline bus services from each of these regions are excellent, and there are also extensive and reliable bus services (both express and those serving local communities) within the Peak District. Several train routes serve the area and the one from Sheffield to Manchester via the Hope Valley is particularly convenient for reaching Edale and Hathersage.

The Peak District National Park and Derbyshire County Council have done much to encourage the greater use of buses and trains with their Backing Public Transport campaign. The County Council's public transport unit publishes an excellent and well cross-referenced timetable of bus and train services in and to the Peak District and this is probably one of the best investments that any serious walker in the Peak District could make. Details of the extensive bus and train services serving each of the route's 10 overnight stopping places are provided in the summary of information at the start of each walking stage.

Taxi services

Taxi and hire-car services may supplement this public transport network and a selective list is provided in Table 7. Local taxi-drivers appear to be well aware of walkers' needs and purses! The normal rate during 1994/5 was about £1 per mile(1.6 km) – a cost which should be acceptable to most walkers, particularly when shared. Of course, if you have to call out a taxi late at night or before the cock crows, do take the precaution of clearly establishing the rate of charge beforehand.

TABLE 7 **TAXI SERVICES**

Location	Name	Phone Number
Ashbourne	Greenway Cars	01335 342964
Bakewell	Ray Downing	01629 812894
	Aitch's Private Hire	01629 813774
Calver	Valley Private Hire	01433 631407
Castleton	Eyre Travel	01433 620983
Hayfield	J. T. Middleton	01663 743505
Longnor	Naden's Taxi	01298 83205
	Lownde's Taxi	01298 83583
Matlock	Weekender Private Hire	01629 584050
Rowsley	Derrick's Cabs	01629 734860
	B. C. Private Hire	01629 732984

Private vehicles

Several major roads cross the Peak District and these, together with connecting spur roads, provide good communication links with all the villages chosen for either starting an individual stage of the walk or passing through during the complete route.

Users of private vehicles have not been neglected by the Peak District authorities. Those walkers attempting one stage of the route at a time should be able to find convenient parking spaces in either a dedicated car park or a lay-by. However, many of these are extremely popular, especially at weekends and on bank holidays, so get there early.

Overnight parking is not generally allowed in public car parks. If you are undertaking the route in one go, make arrangements with the proprietors of the first or last night's accommodation to park vehicles at that establishment or nearby for the entire period.

Increasingly, private firms are offering transport services to long-distance walkers whereby they will carry your equipment between daily starting and finishing locations. Walkers who use such services should ensure that they carry with them all essential items which might be needed on each stage of the walk and should be careful to use only reputable and highly recommended operators. The loss or delay of clothing or gear in transit could upset or ruin the whole itinerary.

Manifold Valley from above Thor's Cave

TABLE 8 **ACCOMMODATION REGISTER**

Key to abbreviations F = Family; D = Double; T = Twin; S = Single.
B&B = Bed and Breakfast; DB&B = Dinner, Bed and Breakfast.
The room charges shown are per person per night.

STAGE 1 – Edale to Hathersage   Overnight stop at Edale

Hotel/Guest House/ Farm	Location Map Ref.	Number of Rooms		Charges/night (£)		Packed Lunch (£)	Open
		En suite	Other	B&B	DB&B		
Mrs Judith Shirt Ladybooth Hall Farm Edale via Sheffield S30 2ZH Tel: 01433 670282	142861	F D T S	F 1 D 1 T 1 S 1	14	20	2.50	Jan to Nov
Mrs M F Elrington Edale House Hope Road Edale via Sheffield S30 2ZE Tel: 01433 670399	130852	F D T 2 S	F D T S 1	17–22		2–3	All year
J E Chapman Brookfield Barber Booth Edale via Sheffield S30 2ZL Tel: 01433 670227	113847	F D T S	F D 1 T 1 S	14		On request	Mar to Oct
Mrs J Beney The Old Parsonage Grindsbrook Edale via Sheffield S30 2ZD Tel: 01433 670232	122860	F D T S	F D 1 T 1 S 1	12.50		On request	Mar to Oct
Julia Reed Stonecroft Edale via Sheffield S30 2ZA Tel: 01433 670262	122854	F D 1 T 1 S	F D 1 T S 1	21	26–36	2.75	All year
Mrs S R Favell Skinners Hall Edale via Sheffield S30 2ZE Tel: 01433 670281		F D 1 T 1 S	F D T S	20–23	By arrange- ment		All year
Mrs Theresa Skillen Ollerbrook Barn Edale via Sheffield S30 2ZG Tel: 01433 670200	128859	F 1 D 1 T S	F D T S	15–21	22–31	2.50	All year

TABLE 8 **ACCOMMODATION REGISTER**

STAGE 1 – Edale to Hathersage   Overnight stop at Edale (continued)

Hotel/Guest House/ Farm	Location Map Ref.	Number of Rooms En suite	Other	Charges/night (£) B&B	DB&B	Packed Lunch (£)	Open
The Rambler Inn Edale via Sheffield S30 2ZA Tel: 01433 670268	122854	F D T S	F 3 D 2 T 3 S	18.50	27	On request	All year

STAGES: 1 & 2 – Edale to Hathersage to Baslow   Overnight stop at Hathersage

Hotel/Guest House/ Farm	Location Map Ref.	Number of Rooms En suite	Other	Charges/night (£) B&B	DB&B	Packed Lunch (£)	Open
Mrs C A B Colley Sladen Jaggers Lane Hathersage via Sheffield S30 1AZ Tel: 01433 650706	227815	F D T S	F 1 D 1 T 1 S	16.50		On request	All year
Mrs E Veevers Moorgate Castleton Road Hathersage via Sheffield S30 1AH Tel: 01433 650293	227814	F D T S	F D 1 T 1 S 1	14–16		2 On request	All year
Mrs M Venning The Old Vicarage Church Bank Hathersage via Sheffield S30 1AB Tel: 01433 651099	234818	F D 1 T S	F D 1 T 1 S	16–20			All year
Mrs A Ward The Mount Castleton Road Hathersage via Sheffield S30 1AH Tel: 01433 650388	227814	F D T S	F D 1 T 2 S	16–18			All year
J E Wilcockson Hillfoot Farm Castleton Road Hathersage via Sheffield S30 1AH Tel: 01433 651673	228814	F 1 D 2 T 2 S	F D T S	17–18	26–27		All year

TABLE 8 **ACCOMMODATION REGISTER**

STAGES: 1 & 2 – Edale to Hathersage to Baslow   Overnight stop at Hathersage (continued)

Hotel/Guest House/ Farm	Location Map Ref.	Number of Rooms		Charges/night (£)		Packed Lunch (£)	Open
		En suite	Other	B&B	DB&B		
Mrs V J Higgins Hilcote Jaggers Lane Hathersage via Sheffield S30 1AZ Tel: 01433 650370	225816	F D T S	F D 2 T 1 S	14			All year
Mrs B Elliott Copperfield Back Lane Hathersage via Sheffield S30 1AR Tel: 01433 650277		F D T S	F 1 D 1 T 1 S	15			
Mrs Hill Salisbury Land End Farm Abney Hathersage via Sheffield S30 1AA Tel: 01433 650371	199799	F D 1 T S	F D 1 T 1 S	16–25		3	All year

STAGES: 2 & 3 – Hathersage to Baslow to Winster   Overnight stop at Baslow

Hotel/Guest House/ Farm	Location Map Ref.	Number of Rooms		Charges/night (£)		Packed Lunch (£)	Open
		En suite	Other	B&B	DB&B		
Mrs Ruth Evans The Fountain House Hydro Close Baslow Derbyshire DE45 1SH Tel: 01246 582156	257726	F D T S	F D 1 T 1 S 1	12–15		2.50	Jan to Nov
Mr and Mrs Gordon Smeeton Selbourne Cottage Bar Road Baslow Derbyshire DE45 1SF Tel: 01246 583142		F D T 1 S	F D T S	15			
Mrs J White Rose Hill Farm Overend Baslow Derbyshire DE45 1SG Tel: 01246 583280	257726	F D T S	F D 1 T 1 S	12.50 –14			Jan to Nov

TABLE 8 ACCOMMODATION REGISTER

STAGES: 2 & 3 – Hathersage to Baslow to Winster   Overnight stop as Baslow (continued)

Hotel/Guest House/ Farm	Location Map Ref.	Number of Rooms		Charges/night (£)		Packed Lunch (£)	Open
		En suite	Other	B&B	DB&B		
Mrs Sue Mills Bubnell Cliff Farm Wheatlands Lane Baslow Derbyshire DE45 1RH Tel: 01246 582454	242718	F D T S	F 1 D 1 T S	14			All year
The Wheatsheaf Nether Road Baslow Derbyshire DE45 1SR Tel: 01246 582240	258722	F D 2 T 1 S	F D T 2 S	17.5– 20	Bar meals		All year
Devonshire Arms Nether End Baslow Derbyshire DE45 1SR Tel: 0246 582551	258722	F 2 D 2 T 8 S 1	F D T S	17–33	Bar meals and Restaurant		All year

STAGES: 3 & 4 – Baslow to Winster to Monyash   Overnight stop at Winster

Hotel/Guest House/ Farm	Location Map Ref.	Number of Rooms		Charges/night (£)		Packed Lunch (£)	Open
		En suite	Other	B&B	DB&B		
Mrs Helen Bastin The Dower House Main Street Winster Nr Matlock DE4 2DH Tel: 01629 650213	243606	F D 1 T 2 S	F D T S	18–28		3	Mar to Oct
Jean and Brian Skyrme Old Shoulder of Mutton West Bank Winster Nr Matlock DE4 2DQ Tel: 01629 650778	240605	F D T S	F D 1 T 1 S	12–13	By arrange- ment	2	All year
Mrs C Rigby Tearsall Farm Bonsall Lane Winster Nr Matlock DE4 2PD Tel: 01629 650602	262599	F D T S	F D 1 T S	12–15			Mar to Oct

TABLE 8 **ACCOMMODATION REGISTER**

STAGES: 3 & 4 – Baslow to Winster to Monyash   Overnight stop at Winster (continued)

Hotel/Guest House/ Farm	Location Map Ref.	Number of Rooms		Charges/night (£)		Packed Lunch (£)	Open
		En suite	Other	B&B	DB&B		
D C MacBain Brae Cottage East Bank Winster Nr Matlock DE4 2DT Tel: 01629 650375		F 1 D 1 T S	F D T S	14			

STAGES: 4 & 5 – Winster to Monyash to Ilam/Thorpe   Overnight stop at Monyash

Hotel/Guest House/ Farm	Location Map Ref.	Number of Rooms		Charges/night (£)		Packed Lunch (£)	Open
		En suite	Other	B&B	DB&B		
Mr and Mrs R H Tyler Sheldon House Chapel Street Monyash Nr Bakewell DE45 1JJ Tel: 01629 813067	150666	F D 3 T S	F D T S	18–21			All year
Mrs Sheila Allen Shuttle Hill Cottage Chapel Street Monyash Nr Bakewell DE45 1JJ Tel: 01629 813979	150666	F D 1 T S	F D 1 T S	16–18			All year
Mr Gary Mycock Chainley Lodge Rowson House Farm Monyash Nr Bakewell DE45 1JH Tel: 01629 813521	152666	F D 1 T S	F D 1 T 1 S 1	14–18			All year
Mrs H J Boam Endmoor House Monyash Nr Bakewell DE45 1JP Tel: 01298 83442		F 1 D 1 T S	F D T S	15			

TABLE 8 **ACCOMMODATION REGISTER**

STAGES: 5 & 6 – Monyash to Ilam/Thorpe to Longnor   Overnight stop at Ilam/Thorpe

Hotel/Guest House/ Farm	Location Map Ref.	Number of Rooms		Charges/night (£)		Packed Lunch (£)	Open
		En suite	Other	B&B	DB&B		
Mrs Marion Hanley Hillcrest House Dovedale, Thorpe Nr Ashbourne Derbyshire DE6 2AW Tel: 01335 350436	153506	F 1 D 3 T 1 S	F D T 1 S 1	18–20	30	Yes	All year
Mrs Sue Prince Beechenhill Farm Dovedale, Ilam Nr Ashbourne Derbyshire DE6 2BD Tel: 01335 310274	131512	F 1 D 1 T S	F D T S	17–22			Mar to Dec
Mrs M A Richardson Throwley Hall Farm Dovedale, Ilam Nr Ashbourne Derbyshire DE6 2BB Tel: 01538 308202/308243	110526	F 1 D 1 T S	F D 1 T 1 S	16–20			Jan to Nov
Mrs B Challinor The Old Orchard Stoney Lane Dovedale, Thorpe Nr Ashbourne DE6 2AW Tel: 01335 350410	155504	F D 2 T S	F D T S 2	17–20			Mar to Nov
Mrs J Brookfield Green Gables Dovedale, Thorpe Nr Ashbourne Derbyshire DE6 2AW Tel: 01335 350386	155504	F D 1 T 1 S	F D 1 T S	20			Feb to Nov
Mr F Gould St Leonard's Cottage Dovedale, Thorpe Nr Ashbourne Derbyshire DE6 2AW Tel: 01335 350224	155504	F D 1 T 1 S 2	F D T S	20			All year

TABLE 8 **ACCOMMODATION REGISTER**

STAGES: 6 & 7 – Ilam/Thorpe to Longnor to Tideswell   Overnight stop at Longnor

Hotel/Guest House/ Farm	Location Map Ref.	Number of Rooms		Charges/night (£)		Packed Lunch (£)	Open
		En suite	Other	B&B	DB&B		
The Crew & Harpur Arms Hotel Longnor Nr Buxton Derbyshire SK17 0NT Tel: 01298 83205	089649	F 4 D 2 T S	F D 1 T S	14–16	Dining room Bar meals	3	All year
The Olde Cheshire Cheese Longnor Nr Buxton Derbyshire SK17 0NS Tel: 01298 83218	089649	F D T S	F 2 D 1 T S	15	Restaurant and bar meals	3	All year
The Grapes Hotel Market Place Longnor Nr Buxton Derbyshire SK17 0NS Tel: 01298 83891	089649	F D T S	F D 1 T 3 S	13–15	Bar meals	3	All Year
Mrs Beresford Underhill Farm, Buxton Road Longnor, Nr Buxton Derbyshire SK17 0PLI Tel: 01298 83281	089655	F D T S	F D 2 T S	15	By arrange- ment	3	Apr to Nov
Mrs Ditchburn Top Farm Sheen, Longnor Nr Buxton Derbyshire Tel: 01298 83271		F D T S	F D T 2 S	13–15	Evening meals	3	All year

STAGES: 7 & 8 – Longnor to Tideswell to Castleton   Overnight stop at Tideswell (or Litton)

Hotel/Guest House/ Farm	Location Map Ref.	Number of Rooms		Charges/night (£)		Packed Lunch (£)	Open
		En suite	Other	B&B	DB&B		
Poppies Bank Square Tideswell Nr Buxton Derbyshire SK17 8LA Tel: 01298 871083	152757	F D 1 T S	F 1 D T 1 S	16–18	25/27	4	Feb to Dec

TABLE 8 **ACCOMMODATION REGISTER**

STAGES: 7 & 8 – Longnor to Tideswell to Castleton   Overnight stop at Tideswell (or Litton) (continued)

Hotel/Guest House/ Farm	Location Map Ref.	Number of Rooms		Charges/night (£)		Packed Lunch (£)	Open
		En suite	Other	B&B	DB&B		
Mrs Jean Bell Laburnum House Sherwood Road Tideswell Nr Buxton Derbyshire SK17 8LH Tel: 01298 872317		F D T S	F D 2 T S 1	14.50– 15.50			
Mrs Pat Harris Laurel House, The Green Litton, Tideswell Nr Buxton Derbyshire SK17 8QP Tel: 01298 871971	165750	F D 1 T S	F D T 1 S	16–20			
Mrs Janet Parsons Beacon House Litton, Tideswell Nr Buxton Derbyshire SK17 8QP Tel: 01298 871752	East of Village	F D 2 T S	F D T S	16.50– 19			
Mrs M Berresford Windrush House, Stemdale Close Litton, Tideswell Nr Buxton Derbyshire SK17 8QZ Tel: 01298 871640		F D T S	F 1 D 1 T S 1	15			

STAGES: 8 & 9 – Tideswell to Castleton to Hayfield   Overnight stop at Castleton

Hotel/Guest House/ Farm	Location Map Ref.	Number of Rooms		Charges/night (£)		Packed Lunch (£)	Open
		En suite	Other	B&B	DB&B		
Mrs P D M Gillott Ramblers Rest Back Street, Millbridge Castleton via Sheffield S30 2WR Tel: 01433 620125	150831	F 1 D 3 T 2 S 1	F D 2 T S	15–20		On request	All year

TABLE 8 **ACCOMMODATION REGISTER**

STAGES: 8 & 9 – Tideswell to Castleton to Hayfield   Overnight stop at Castleton (continued)

Hotel/Guest House/ Farm	Location Map Ref.	Number of Rooms		Charges/night (£)		Packed Lunch (£)	Open
		En suite	Other	B&B	DB&B		
Kelseys Swiss House How Lane Castleton via Sheffield S30 2WJ Tel: 01433 621098	153831	F 1 D 5 T 3 S 1	F D T S	22.50	34		All year
Mrs E M Marsden The Lodge Back Street Castleton via Sheffield S30 2WE Tel: 01433 620526	150828	F D T S	F 1 D 2 T S 1	16– 17			Mar to Dec
S and D Newsome Bargate Cottage Market Place Castleton via Sheffield S30 2WG Tel: 01433 620201	150828	F D 2 T 1 S	F D T S	19– 22	29–32	2	All year
Mrs P J Webster Hillside House Pindale Road Castleton via Sheffield S30 2WU Tel: 01433 620312	151827	F D 1 T S	F 1 D T 1 S	17– 18.50			All year
Mr and Mrs T Skelton Cryer House Castleton via Sheffield S30 2WG Tel: 01433 620244	149829	F D T S	F 1 D 2 T S	15		2.50/3.50	All year
Mrs B Johnson Myrtle Cottage Market Place Castleton via Sheffield S30 2WQ Tel: 01433 620787	150828	F 2 D 3 T S	F D T S	18		2.50	Feb to Nov
The Castle Hotel Castle Street Castleton via Sheffield S30 2WG Tel: 01433 620578	149829	F D 7 T 2 S	F D T S	30–40	Restaurant and bar meals	4	All year

TABLE 8 **ACCOMMODATION REGISTER**

STAGES: 8 & 9 – Tideswell to Castleton to Hayfield   Overnight stop at Castleton (continued)

Hotel/Guest House/ Farm	Location Map Ref.	Number of Rooms		Charges/night (£)		Packed Lunch (£)	Open
		En suite	Other	B&B	DB&B		
The Old Nag's Head Castleton via Sheffield S30 2WH Tel: 01433 620248	150828	F D 6 T 2 S	F D T S	26–42	Restaurant and bar meals	On request	All year

STAGES 9 & 10 – Castleton to Hayfield to Edale   Overnight stop at Hayfield

Hotel/Guest House/ Farm	Location Map Ref.	Number of Rooms		Charges/night (£)		Packed Lunch (£)	Open
		En suite	Other	B&B	DB&B		
Sheila Collier Johnson The Old Bank House Hayfield Derbyshire SK12 5EP Tel: 01663 747354	038870	F D T S	F 1 D 2 T 1 S	20	30	3.50	All year
Mr and Mrs T Abbotts Fox Hall Barn Kinder Road Hayfield Derbyshire SK12 5HS Tel: 01663 745090	039869	F D T S	F D 1 T 1 S	20			All year
G and B Tier Bridge End Restaurant 7 Church Street Hayfield Derbyshire SK12 5JE Tel: 01663 747321	038869	F 1 D 2 T 1 S	F D T S	20			All year
The Royal Hotel Market Street Hayfield Derbyshire SK12 5EP Tel: 01663 742721	038870	F 1 D 1 T 1 S	F D T S	20–25	27–32	On request	All year
Mrs Pat Isaacs Stet Barn Farm Little Hayfield Derbyshire SK12 5NS Tel: 01663 745970	North of Hayfield Village	F D 1 T 1 S	F D T S	17			Feb to Dec

APPENDIX: STATISTICS

The 10 stages of the prescribed route provide, in total, over 100 miles of challenging hill walking. They also involve a total height gain of over 12 000ft, mostly climbing unrelenting slopes or scaling steep-sided gorges. The distance walked is roughly equivalent to half the journey from Manchester to London whilst the height gained is approaching the altitude of the infamous Eiger Mountain in the Alps.

The time allowances, distances and heights for the 10 stages are summarized in Table 9, and presented graphically in Table 10. The statistics in Table 9 cover each separate stage, and cumulative figures are also given for all the stages completed up to the end of each successive stage.

TABLE 9 **SUMMARY OF TIME ALLOWANCES, DISTANCES WALKED AND HEIGHTS CLIMBED**

Stage	Individual Stages					Cumulative				
	Time allowance	Distance walked (including height)		Height climbed		Time allowance	Distance walked (including height)		Height climbed	
	Hours	Km	Miles	M	Feet	Hours	Km	Miles	M	Feet
1 EDALE to HATHERSAGE	7.0	18.6	11.5	590	1935	7.0	18.6	11.5	590	1935
2 HATHERSAGE to BASLOW	6.5	18.5	11.5	390	1280	13.5	37.1	23.0	980	3215
3 BASLOW to WINSTER	6.0	16.0	9.9	420	1375	19.5	53.1	32.9	1400	4590
4 WINSTER to MONYASH	6.0	17.8	11.1	200	655	25.5	70.9	44.0	1600	5245
5 MONYASH to ILAM/THORPE	6.5	21.4	13.3	150	490	32.0	92.3	57.3	1750	5735
6 ILAM/THORPE to LONGNOR	7.0	20.1	12.5	330	1080	39.0	112.4	69.8	2080	6815
7 LONGNOR to TIDESWELL	6.5	17.7	11.0	410	1345	45.5	130.1	80.8	2490	8160
8 TIDESWELL to CASTLETON	5.0	12.9	8.0	250	820	50.5	143.0	88.8	2740	8980
9 CASTLETON to HAYFIELD	5.5	14.8	9.2	450	1475	56.0	157.8	98.0	3190	10455
10 HAYFIELD to EDALE	6.0	14.1	8.8	560	1835	62.0	171.9	106.8	3750	12290
	62.0	171.9	106.8	3750	12290					

TABLE 10 **DISTANCE WALKED (including height)**

STAGE

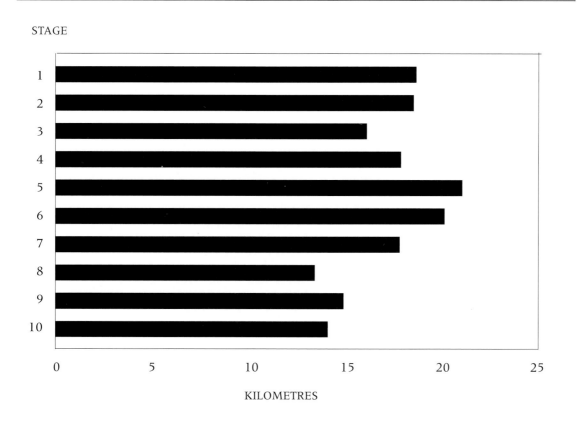

KILOMETRES

TABLE 11 **HEIGHT CLIMBED**

METRES

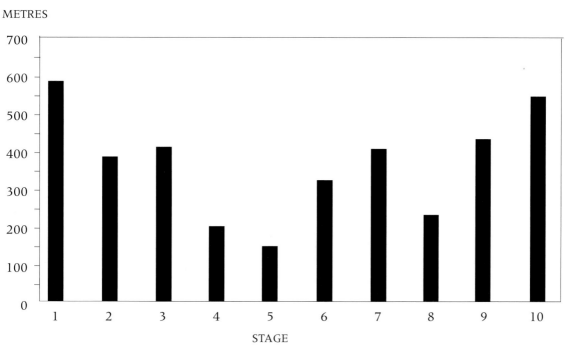

STAGE

INDEX